WHO I AM
AFTER ALL

a memoir by

JEFF ANSELL

 FriesenPress

One Printers Way
Altona, MB R0G 0B0
Canada

www.friesenpress.com

ISBN
978-1-03-910844-8 (Hardcover)
978-1-03-910843-1 (Paperback)
978-1-03-910845-5 (eBook)

1. BIOGRAPHY & AUTOBIOGRAPHY, EDITORS, JOURNALISTS, PUBLISHERS

Distributed to the trade by The Ingram Book Company

I started to sob uncontrollably—
afraid I wouldn't be coming home from the hospital.

All I could think was that I wanted one more time.

One more time to hug my grandkids.

One more time for a family vacation.

One more time...

DEDICATION

For my wonderful wife and life partner Annie, whose beautiful eyes captivated me the moment we met. Your love and encouragement support me in all aspects of our lives together, and I can only hope I do the same for you.

You truly are one of a kind, and I'm so grateful you married me. Thank you, Annie.

For my devoted sons Josh and Adam, and Adam's sweet wife Liana, who look up to me despite my many flaws. And for my beautiful grandkids Mia and Jake, who will discover their grandfather is a little too human.

TABLE OF CONTENTS

FOREWORD
by Dr. Jack Muskat

It is not often that you get a second chance to write a foreword for a friend whose first memoir I commented on so critically that I thought I would never hear from him again.

But this is Jeff. Uncompromisingly honest. With himself. With others, except when—well, you'll read about it.

When Jeff asked me to read his manuscript, it was with the following caveat: "As a psychologist, you know how to pull stuff out of people, things that they may not even recognize about themselves. Is the book honest?" Jeff wanted to know. "Don't pull any punches." A daunting task, indeed.

Can we ever *really* know anyone? And what does "honest" mean in an age of "fake news?" To top it off, Jeff himself is a master of the spin and PR genre, having spent the latter half of his career as a highly sought-after crisis management expert and media advisor to some of the world's most powerful political and business leaders.

If I had known how many great stories he has, celebrities he knows, and world leaders he has met and worked with, I would have been much nicer to him. Sorry, Jeff.

I expected this book to be another vanity project with the dark spots photoshopped out. Instead, I was treated to a remarkable story told with astonishing candor and clarity. Whereas Jeff's original book that I panned was written in his "radio" voice, here we get the real Jeff, speaking his genuine voice.

We visit Jeff from his humble beginnings in Jewish working-class Montreal—the same community that spawned Mordecai Richler and William Shatner, and where his father toiled lifelong in Leonard Cohen's family's garment factory. Jeff's later career as a media adviser and trainer brought him face to face with executives responsible for some of the worst disasters in history.

All of the above is commendable—gripping prose, high drama, and big stakes.

What struck me most about this book, and more importantly, about Jeff, is how vulnerable his life was and still is. He tells of his frightening panic attacks that cropped up at the worst of times in his media career and are the death knell for a public speaking expert.

He has struggled with guilt over his mother's death, his own health concerns, and his doubts about his adequacy as a father of two boys, now grown men, and as husband to his steadfast wife, Annie, who has stood by him through it all.

Jeff does not gloss over any of it. His story is told without an ounce of self-pity or excuse.

As the stories progress, we start to see a pattern emerge. From Jeff, the "frightened little boy" whose driving ambition, work ethic, and "street smarts" overcame his insecurities and shame, to Jeff, the crusading journalist and globe-trotting advisor to leaders in crisis. The pattern is simply this: Jeff is driven by the need to always do right by people, whatever the cost, and to remember the little guy even when he is the big guy himself.

Even more surprising is his inestimable courage and strength of character in facing down his demons. That is the real lesson of this book.

We can all learn from these stories of life that we are all linked by our common desire to find meaning and purpose in our lives, to help others, to be well regarded, and to not screw things up.

That's Jeff's story. It is our story, too.

Jack Muskat, PhD, is a Toronto-based organizational and clinical psychologist, writer, and lecturer with over twenty-five years of consulting and business experience with individuals and organizations. Dr. Muskat is an acknowledged expert on issues relating to organizational culture and leadership, as well as mental health and emotional well-being.
jack@drjackmuskat.com

INTRODUCTION

Why have I written this book, and why would anyone want to read it? After all, who am I?

Career-wise, my role has been to tell stories and help people be better communicators. Aside from a few personal and professional achievements, I'm not particularly famous or widely well known. Yet, when I share my stories, people inevitably tell me to write a book about them.

For years, I've thought about writing a book about my many life experiences. However, I'm mindful of what Jerry Seinfeld said about people *thinking* of writing a book. According to Jerry, someone who says they are *thinking* about writing a book will never do it. Well, I'm calling Jerry's bluff.

I did write a book previously on how best to communicate with media, especially during a crisis. I'm grateful the book, entitled *When the Headline Is You: An Insider's Guide to Handling the Media,* became an Amazon bestseller in the Public Relations category.

But this book is different. Very different.

This is actually my second attempt at writing a book documenting my personal experiences in life, which up to now have mostly been private, and in some cases, extraordinary. My first, never-published book of life experiences was called *What's in Your Heart.*

I asked my good friend Jack, who graciously wrote the foreword to this book, to read the manuscript because I knew Jack would be honest with me. He was actually too honest.

Jack told me that some writers take lousy stories and turn them into great ones. He said I took great stories and turned them into lousy ones. He was right.

That initial book of my life experiences was total crapola. I wrote that manuscript after triple bypass heart surgery and was clearly in a touchy-feely frame of mind. Looking at it now—what I wrote then feels pithy and inauthentic. Plus, I held back on telling too much of the truth for fear of revealing that which I've never talked about to anyone before.

Then, when I got cancer, I wanted another shot at telling my stories, including those of which I'm ashamed. *Who I Am After All* is the result.

Over the course of my nearly fifty-year career, I've encountered a fascinating parade of characters. This book is, simply, a mix of what I hope are interesting tales with a background as to how some of them unfolded.

Jane Fonda (whom I briefly met and was nicer than I expected) once said, "If you want to know how to go forward, you need to know where you've been." With that in mind, here's why I wrote this book.

When I was diagnosed with cancer, I thought I might die. I wanted to tell my stories before that happened, mostly for my loved ones so they'll know more of the true me and the person I wanted to be, yet often wasn't.

I also wrote this book because my experiences have been so vast and all-encompassing—I thought others might truly be interested in some of my stories.

The third reason I wrote this book is because I've experienced my fair share of stress, struggles, and setbacks. Though this is by no means a self-help book, one or two of my stories may resonate with someone—hopefully in a positive way. Plus, the steps I took to be more than I was may be of value to a few others as well.

In creating this book, some stories I tell are personal—deeply personal—and they don't all make me look good. The stories include disturbing childhood memories, investigations I worked on as a reporter, individuals who influenced me, plus thoughts on celebrities I interviewed and, by happenstance, bumped into over the years. You see, I have a propensity to randomly encounter famous people—some of whom were quite nice, others of whom were jerks. I'll name names.

What follows are some of the moments, stories, and adventures that stand out over the years.

Like how I became an instructor at Harvard University, which is quite remarkable considering that I'm a high school dropout.

As you read my stories, I hope my occasional shift from dark stories to lighter ones and then back again isn't too jarring.

Then again, if in the end, the only ones who read this are my family, I'll be more than happy. Though, the kids may still be a little too young to hear about their grandfather's arrest in San Francisco.

I'll share the story anyway.

I'll even share my story about Jerry Seinfeld.

CHAPTER ONE

Who I Am

My name is Jeffrey Ansel.

I grew up with a huge inferiority complex.

My father smacked me a lot when I was growing up—often, if not always, for next to nothing. Once, my father hit me because I bought a shirt made in China and not in North America. That slap took place in my grandmother's living room, with people all around to witness.

Another time, while preparing lunch in the kitchen on a Saturday afternoon, he walloped me for "wasting" my seventy-five-cent allowance on a cheap ring I bought that morning in a variety store.

Once, when I had a friend over, my father screamed at me for wearing flip-flops instead of regular shoes. That's partly why I was afraid to bring friends to my apartment when my father was home—because I never knew when he would blow up and yell or hit me in front of them.

"You're a dummy," he often told me. Deep down, I knew I wasn't really a dummy. My marks throughout my school years were always high, and I didn't really feel stupid. Still, I lived in near-constant fear that people could tell that I felt less than whole and less than others.

Being embarrassed publicly was a big issue for me as a boy. Being embarrassed made me feel small—not wanting to be noticed. Despite numerous occurrences of physical and emotional bullying, the single incident that stands out took place before my bar mitzvah.

We had a dinner for family and out-of-towners at the Brown Derby restaurant, a popular Montreal deli with moderate prices. There must have been at least a dozen of us sitting at the table, enjoying our time together. For me, being in a restaurant as a kid was always a big deal. It was a real treat.

Me and the other kids at the table were fooling around. We were having fun, mischievously pouring ketchup into our water glasses, when I accidentally spilled some onto the adult next to me.

While looking at the stain I had caused, my father angrily thwacked me in the face in front of everyone. Then, he threatened me: "Smarten up, or you'll eat your supper alone in the toilet!"

Other youngsters at the table thought that was funny and laughed. I was humiliated in front of an audience, including servers and strangers at nearby tables. Even now, when I'm reminded of that dinner, a cousin still chuckles, because to him, what my father said was funny. He didn't understand the hurtful impact that memory continues to have on me.

As a boy desperately in need of real confidence, I read and re-read self-help books like *The Power of Positive Thinking* by Norman Vincent Peale and devoured human psychology books like *I'm OK – You're OK* by Thomas Anthony Harris. Books like those made me feel better about myself—if only for a brief while.

Sometimes though, the benefits of self-help books were offset by the sensation that I was trapped in a tiny space, unable to get out.

I have a memory that I'm not sure is real. I may have experienced it in a dream, if not in real life. In that memory or dream, my father locked me in our apartment building's dark, cramped incinerator room because I misbehaved. When I pulled open the incinerator chute to look inside, flames shot up from the basement, the source of the fire, with sparks everywhere. I was scared. Again, I don't know if that ever happened.

All I wanted as a youngster was to feel better about myself and escape from the fears I felt, to be free of the uncertainty of when I'd be hit and embarrassed again.

I didn't want to be like those who'd hurt me.

Over the years, I've wanted to be a good husband and a good father, yet often failed on those critically important fronts.

Annie, thankfully, understands and tolerates that I am a man with a great many faults, and I am deeply grateful for her love.

It's said that when we grow up, we either copy the strong behaviors of our parents or else go in the opposite direction. Even now, when I see somebody being embarrassed, especially by a parent or family member—I relate. That's why I will never knowingly embarrass another human being.

Though it's a rule for me now, I'm guilty of having done it myself—to my own kids. In my early years of parenting, I sometimes treated my boys in a less-than-respectful fashion, and today I am sorry for that as well.

I remember when one of my sons was eight years old. We were at a movie theatre and he didn't know which size drink to get. "Dad, should I get the medium or the large?"

"Figure it out for yourself," I barked.

Here he was, looking to me for some guidance over something so simple, but I was snarky in return. You were just a little boy. I'm sorry I snapped at you.

Or the Saturday we came home from synagogue and there wasn't enough food on the table for everybody. You grabbed what you liked and didn't want to share it—then I yelled at you angrily in front of everybody.

There were many moments when I should have known better but didn't. Instead of being thoughtful—I was the opposite. I thoughtlessly chastised you in front of others. I'm sorry, and I'm ashamed.

These incidents may sound incidental or trite, but not to me. I know what's it like to feel embarrassed, and I don't like it.

These days, if there's a room full of people and the law of averages says someone in the room must be embarrassed—I insist it be me. I never want to inflict that feeling on anyone unless it helps a situation or a life lesson results from it.

Instead of embarrassing others, there are better ways to handle delicate issues and matters.

> *I'm sorry for all the times I not only embarrassed others, but also didn't jump in to help others captured in that moment.*

My Parents...

Me, my father Moe, mother Beatrice, and two older sisters, Dina and Eileen, lived in a lower-middle-class part of Montreal. We had a small, third floor walk-up apartment. The incinerator room was directly across from our apartment's front door, three feet away.

Eileen, five years older than me, had to share a bedroom with her baby brother until she was in her mid-teens, which was when Dina married Buzzie and moved to Brooklyn. A girl Eileen's age deserved her privacy—not a brother who, more often than not, was a nuisance. Eileen would tell me otherwise, but thinking back, I feel terrible about her lack of personal space.

The rent for our apartment, as I recall, was $120 a month. Can you imagine? That's $4 a day! The four apartments per floor were tightly packed together, so much so, you could smell what everyone was having for supper. Arguments next door could be heard, blasting through the thin walls. Neighbors, no doubt, heard much of the madness that went on in our apartment. There was a lot of yelling in our house, frequently between my parents.

> *Sometimes, Dina and Eileen would be on the receiving end of our father's wrath—though not as often as me, I think. Or at least, I hope. I can't say for certain because it's not something the three of us have ever talked about.*

My friends, meanwhile, lived in homes—some of which were like mansions to me. We never had a car either, which I was kind of embarrassed about. Most everybody we knew had a car—except us.

We took the bus almost everywhere we went. When we weren't riding the bus, we were dependent on others to get places. I never liked that feeling of having to depend on others for something as basic as getting around.

Could my parents have afforded a car? I don't know. I just knew we didn't have one. When I asked my father why we didn't have a car, he'd reply, "We drive around in the most expensive vehicle there is—a bus."

I would just look at friends who had more than me and think that anyone who lived in a house and had a car was a millionaire.

I was very close to my mother. When I was really young, after my father would leave for work, I would crawl into bed next to her. It was comforting.

Together, we would listen to the music and morning news on the radio, and then she would get up for work while I got ready for school.

At bedtime, my mother would come to my bedside to make sure I recited the Shema. The Shema is a Hebrew prayer that declares the oneness of G-d. It's a prayer I said every morning and night as a child, and still do.

I loved my mother dearly. I couldn't say the same about my father.

When I was about nine years old, we had a Father's Day project at school. We took small, empty boxes and wrote a message on them using macaroni lettering. The box was to store tchotchkes.

Most kids used the macaroni to write "Happy Father's Day—I love you, Dad." I couldn't do that.

I wrote, "Happy Father's Day—I like you, Dad."

Thinking back, I'm not certain even that was true at the time.

In Search of Confidence...

As a youngster, I found inspiration from Mark Twain's *Tom Sawyer* and *Huckleberry Finn*, so when actor Hal Holbrook was coming to town to perform in his one-man show, *Mark Twain Tonight!*[1] I knew I had to be there.

Tickets were a couple of dollars, and the morning they went on sale, I was first in line to get myself a front-row seat to the show.

Come showtime, I discovered my seat was, in fact, directly in Mark Twain's eyeline and he looked at me the entire evening. Being an insecure kid, the fact that "Mark Twain" was staring directly at me pumped me up, making me feel important.

From that experience, I'm always mindful of how we can connect with others simply by using our eyes, as Mark Twain connected with me. It's a testament to Hal Holbrook's acting ability that probably every single person in that auditorium must have felt the same.

But no matter. That night I knew he was looking at only one person, me—Jeffrey Ansel—the little kid in the front row.

Discovering Radio...

I remember the precise day radio came into my life. I was ten years old.

A cousin who was three years older than me, also named Jeff, had a tape recorder, the first I had ever seen. Jeff set up the recorder on the living room rug, plugged in the microphone, and together we sprawled out on the carpet, pretending we were radio announcers. Jeff was the disc jockey who introduced the music.

> *At the time, I remember wondering how real radio stations got all those musicians in and out of their studios so fast when they played the different songs.*

While Jeff played DJ, I was the news announcer. For something to announce, I read from the front page of the newspaper. I still remember that I read about "enemy planes with ruptured belly cockpits." That line made me and Jeff laugh our asses off.

After that experience in Jeff's living room, I was absolutely hooked on radio and got a real kick out of "playing" the news announcer. That's when I started paying more attention to people reading the news on the radio. I knew I wanted to be one of them.

I loved radio so much that on evenings while my family sat in the living room watching TV, I would lie on my parents' bed playing with the radio dial. Nighttime offered the clearest signals on the radio.

My folks had the best radio in the house, and I would listen to faraway radio stations like WABC New York and CHUM Toronto, top stations with the most talented DJs and news broadcasters anywhere.

Though my own voice hadn't even changed yet, I tried to mimic their voices. From my parents' room, even with the door closed, my family would hear me announce: "WABC—most music radio—seventy-seven—New York City."

Because of all that practice, I can still do what I call my "stupid human trick." While listening to a radio or TV or hearing a person talk, I can repeat exactly what they say with barely a quarter-second delay—without knowing what they are going to say ahead of time. I've been honing the ability ever since. Copying others was my way of faking it until I could discover my own unique voice.

As much as I dreamed of being on radio, I still had no idea what a real radio station looked like. Being an obsessed kid, I needed to see the inside of one for myself. I wanted to be in its studios, walk its hallways, and work, one day, in its newsroom. But you couldn't just walk into a radio station and say, "I want to look around." I needed a path to get in.

I contacted CFCF, a top radio and TV station in Montreal. "Can I please come down for a tour of the station?" I asked the station's switchboard operator.

"We don't offer individual tours," she told me. "We may do a special tour for a group, but no one-on-one tours."

"How many people would need to be in a group?" I wondered.

"Ten, at least. Plus, if you're under eighteen, which you clearly are, you'll need a grownup chaperone."

I rounded up the friends, and my mom actually took the day off work, which was a big deal, just so I could get into a radio station. Those three steps—calling the station, finding out about the tours, and gathering a group of friends together, resulted in step four—the tour I hoped for.

Walking through the studios, I was in seventh heaven watching the on-air announcers. In the newsroom, other announcers and reporters were putting together the next newscast. They were clanking on typewriters—pecking away, one finger at a time—the way I still type.

There was a magical feeling in the newsroom—something important was happening, and these were the people about to tell us what it was. The energy was frenetic, and I was so excited to be there to watch.

We were introduced to a few radio hosts on the tour, and I was shocked because none of these announcers looked how I envisioned. Such big voices coming out of ordinary-looking people. (Years later, I was told I had a face for radio—yeah, I know that's an old one.)

CFCF also used to produce television shows in front of live studio audiences. These shows—situation comedies, game shows, and novelty shows on magic, astrology, and the like—were taped on the weekends, and I went to almost every one. I felt a buzz waiting in line to get in, then being ushered into the studio and watching the shows actually being made.

On the radio station tour that day, I discovered for the first time that if a kid like me could finagle his way into a radio station, then just about anything was possible. I'm so glad that I learned early on that you don't get if you don't ask.

Looking into the radio studio, I pictured myself sitting in that same chair, broadcasting the news. Just a few years later, it actually happened.

On My Hands and Knees...

At the age of fifteen, I wanted a real ring—not one for seventy-five cents that would turn my finger purple—but I had no money to buy one.

I couldn't ask my parents for the money, so I got an after-school and weekend job at a nearby grocery store called SPOT Supermarket. My job was to stock shelves, pack groceries at the cash, and carry customers' shopping bags to their cars.

Thankfully, SPOT's wasn't as big as today's grocery superstores because I discovered that part of my job every Saturday at closing time was to scrub seven aisles of floor with peanut oil. We didn't use a mop, just a sponge.

So, each weekend I would be on my hands and knees for hours, scrubbing and oiling the floor from one end of the store to the other. By the end of my shift, my knees used to bleed. More than once, I remember going out on a Saturday night with friends, wearing a nice pair of pants with stains on the knees because I was still bleeding.

My friends didn't know a lot about my family life because I never told them. But they did know I was a hard worker, literally willing to get on my hands and knees to make a buck. Still, I hated my job at SPOT's.

"Dad, I want to quit my job at the supermarket. I can't stand working there anymore."

My father saw SPOT's as a bird in the hand. "Don't be a dummy," he said. "One day, they might make you the manager of the produce department."

"But I don't want to manage the produce department," I told him. I'm not sure he understood.

After six months, I took the money I had made at the supermarket and went to a local jeweler. With his help, I designed a beautiful gold ring with my initials "JA" on it and a very inexpensive but handsome zircon birthstone in the middle. I wear that ring to this day. In the years since, I've replaced the stone with a diamond that my mother inherited and gave to me as a gift.

The ring looks fancier and is worth more now, largely in sentimental value. But when I stop and look at it, that ring still reminds me of SPOT Supermarket—and how I learned as a youngster that just about everything was within reach.

Who I Come From...

Given his history as a worker, it's easy to understand why my father wanted me to have a secure job with a future, modest as it was. His desire for me to stay at SPOT's reflected his own job path.

Moe, or Moishe as his friends called him, was the oldest of four children, the youngest of whom, Eliezer, had died as a child of sunstroke during summer camp. I suspect this is why my parents never allowed me to go to sleepaway camp as a kid.

Eliezer is now my Hebrew middle name. Growing up, I would often wonder if I was Uncle Eliezer's reincarnation. If I was indeed my uncle come back to life, I wondered what—if anything—my special purpose was in coming back.

My grandmother never got over Eliezer's death and understandably became overprotective of my father's siblings. When my father's brother Sammy came home with a pair of ice skates, my grandmother burned them in the oven.

At the height of the Great Depression, Moe was forced to quit school in grade seven to help provide for his family. He took a job at the Freedman Company, a high-end men's clothing factory. It was the same factory where both my grandfathers worked. My father's mother—my grandmother—worked at another nearby factory where she was described as the best button sewer in all of Montreal.

My mother, Beatrice, also known as Bookie, was the second oldest of four daughters. Bookie was a derivative of my mother's Hebrew name Brucha, which means blessing. Bookie began working in the Freedman Company's office after finishing high school at the age of seventeen.

She once told me the story of what Moe did the first time they met. "He chased me around the office," my mom said. I'm not exactly sure what her initial reaction was (it was a picture I couldn't make work in my head), but obviously, it worked.

Bookie & Moe

When I was a kid, my mom worked part-time at the Cadbury chocolate factory, maker of Caramilk, Kit-Kat, and dozens of other candy bar brands. Chocolate bars with imperfections were thrown into a basket. Every week, my mom would come home with a paper bag full of deformed Crunchie and Snack bars—our Friday night treats!

At the end of the working day, my father's greatest pleasure was to take off his shoes and socks and read the newspaper in his undershirt on the balcony. He'd nurse a beer, have supper, then watch TV or play cards with friends.

The Freedman Company was owned by the family of the musician Leonard Cohen. Cohen was born and raised in Westmount, where many really rich Jews lived. Pillars of the community, the Cohens were described by author Michael Posner as "Jewish royalty."

However, the Cohen family treated my father and other employees with disrespect and clearly lacked appreciation for their hard work. My dad worked at the Freedman for more than fifty years—World War Two being his only break—and all he would get for Christmas each year was a stale cake.

Meanwhile, Leonard, the dilettante poet-songster, fluttered around the globe in search of Zen. I grew up with a hate-on for the Freedman Company and Leonard Cohen—though he had nothing to do with the factory itself, only the money it made.

I remember visiting my dad at work one day, watching him hold the most humongous pair of shears I'd ever seen. The shears were used to cut fabric that was turned into men's suits. From the age of thirteen on, my father stood on his feet for nine hours a day, at his worktable, clutching those shears. He was just a boy when he started, barely past his own bar mitzvah.

I was told that as a youngster, Moe was a very good student and had wonderful penmanship. Yet, he gave up his education to support his parents and younger siblings, who later went on to complete high school. In adulthood, my father continued at the Freedman Company, supporting his wife and three kids. That's quite the accomplishment.

My dad cut cloth with those enormous shears until his early sixties when the Freedman Company closed, and he was laid off. Never once, in my entire life, did I hear my father complain. I could never have done what he did—standing, on his feet, in a factory, for more than fifty years.

Every Sunday morning when I was a kid, my dad and I would take the bus to visit his parents, my Bubie and Zaidy. We would all sit together in my grandparents' living room, listening to the old-time radio shows featured on Sunday mornings. Listening to those shows, I would practice my "radio voice," driving my Zaidy nuts. He used to wag his cane at me to get me to shut up.

Bubie would make me bubble (scrambled) eggs for breakfast, while my father tended to Zaidy. Every week for years, my dad carried my Zaidy into the bathroom to bathe him. Again, my father never complained.

He had a younger brother who rarely filled in. Sammy was as different from Moe as can be. Sammy had a loud, gravelly voice and a large personality. He had a successful business and drove a Corvette.

As the eldest, my dad must have seen it as his duty to care for his parents. In the Jewish religion, one of the most important commandments is to honor your mother and father. My dad did just that. As I write this now, I have tears in my eyes. For the first time, I realize that my dad was a wonderful son, and I now see the sacrifices he made on behalf of his family.

Even though he sometimes hit me as a kid, I knew inside that my dad loved me. Sensing he felt bad smacking me, I recall him occasionally trying to atone for it. After he hit me, I would go into my room, get into bed, crawl under the covers, and cry. Every once in a while, he would come into my room and I would pretend to be asleep, not wanting him to talk to me or me to him.

Still, we went to baseball and football games together, played catch a lot, and took surprise bus trips to Brooklyn to visit Dina and Buzz. So, as a boy, I did have some nice moments with my dad.

On many of our long walks (no car), my father would hammer a single message into my head: "Become a professional, like a doctor or lawyer," he would tell me. "Don't be a factory worker."

Do I blame my father for treating me as he did? Yes and no. My guess is he grew up being smacked around by his father and mother, so hitting me became one of his go-to parenting tools. Plus—if my father hadn't treated me the way he did, would I be the same person I am now, presuming that's a positive?

Later in life, Annie and I brought our sons Adam and Josh to Montreal to visit family. After Adam misbehaved, I gently tapped his ass to discipline him. That's when my father said, "Don't hit him."

What did I just hear? Did my old man just tell me not to hit Adam, even with a light pat on the rear end? This, from the guy who used to make a public spectacle of smacking me?

I could not let the moment pass, so I asked my dad, "When I was a kid, did you ever hit me?" He looked down and paused for a moment. "I was a bastard," he admitted.

I wasn't sure what he would say, but I sure didn't expect to hear him say that. His acknowledgment of my mistreatment meant a lot to me—probably to him too, I suspect.

To this day, my dad's shears hang on the wall prominently next to my desk—a daily reminder of where I come from and my working-class roots.

Plus—they remind me of how hard my dad worked. My father's shears are among my most prized possessions.

My father's shears

CHAPTER TWO
Wanting

When I got older and entered the news business, I realized that the way my father had treated me as a kid was a key reason I wanted to be a reporter. It wasn't just to regurgitate daily doings in the news, but also to help everyday people deal with those who would bully or do them harm.

I'm talking about ordinary people like the vulnerable elderly mistreated in nursing homes or patients with doctors who abuse their privilege and power. Like the drug-pushing physicians I later took down and the derelict nursing home I closed.

Reporters—especially those who investigate and dig deeper—look out for people who can't or don't know how to fight back on their own. Investigative journalists like Carl Bernstein and Bob Woodward proved reporters could make a difference in the world.

Watergate came to the fore in 1973, when I was seventeen. Woodward and Bernstein literally changed the course of history. Bad guys need to be busted, and Woodward and Bernstein busted the president of the United States—the most powerful man in the world.

Woodward and Bernstein inspired in me a desire to help right wrongs.

I must admit, I later discovered my motives in wanting to be a radio and TV reporter were not entirely selfless. After all, most reporters on radio and TV have resonant voices.

I thought that maybe if I had a deep voice, people would believe I was strong. Then maybe I'd feel more confident and less inferior than others.

Getting In the Door...

People, mostly friends, told me I had a pretty good radio voice. Despite my lack of confidence or formal training, I knew that I was starting to sound like a real announcer now that my voice had changed.

As young as I was, three years after the CFCF tour, I was accepted as an evening volunteer at Radio Sir George, a station that broadcasted on the Sir George Williams University campus. Sir George Williams created the YMCA.

Here, I was actually on the air several nights a week, playing records, reading news, and operating the control board for others. The fact that few people, if any, were listening didn't matter much, if at all. I was used to practicing in front of an audience of none.

Though I was still in high school, I was now broadcasting along-side much older university students. Sure, they began treating me like a mascot, the one everybody teased and kidded. But the reason they tolerated me at all was because I was pretty good on the radio and sounded a lot older than fifteen.

Again, I realized at an early age that if I wanted something—no one would give it to me. I would need to work for it.

Thirsting for a taste of the big leagues, I also hung around outside CKGM, Montreal's most popular rock radio station. I'd drag my friends Renée and Mayer with me—our goal was to meet a radio announcer; it didn't matter who.

So, we would stand outside the CKGM office building, cup our hands around our eyes, and peer in through the window. Because of the dim light and the darkly shaded window glass, it was hard to see inside the building.

One day, out of the elevator walked this real cool guy with long hair, very funky-looking round glasses, and big bell-bottom pants. Figuring he had to be an announcer, we waited until he walked out the main door.

Clearly taking pity on this kid who hovered with his friends near the doorway, he actually stopped to talk to me. "Hey, what's up?" he asked.

Then we all said excitedly, "Are you on the radio? Are you on the radio?!"

"Yes," he said.

"Who are you? Who are you?"

"I'm Earl Jive."[2]

This wasn't just any announcer; this was *the* "Live Earl Jive," one of the city's top broadcasters. His appearance caught me by surprise, however. Close to a foot shorter than me, with a largish nose—he looked completely different from the picture I had in my head.

I stood there a little stunned.

My friends' enthusiasm brought me back to the moment. "Show him your voice, Jeffrey," shouted Renée.

"I want to be on the radio, too!" I said to Earl.

"Do your radio voice, Jeffrey!" chimed in Mayer.

This was an opportunity I could not pass up—a once-in-a-lifetime, do-or-die moment. The Big Audition—sort of. Knowing that this was my best shot, in my deepest announcer's voice, the one I'd been practicing hour after hour beside the radio, I said, "C-K-G-M—Super 98—I'm Jeffrey Ansel."

Earl laughed. "Hey, not bad!" he said, validating my years of practice. "Want to do some volunteer work at the station?"

What a question!

Earl worked at CHOM FM, CKGM's sister station, both located on the same floor. While CKGM was top 40, CHOM was the more avant-garde, pass the spliff station.

Thanks to that encounter, Earl helped me become an after-school volunteer at both stations. My job was to tape ripped music album jackets and clean dirty ashtrays—back in the days when people were allowed to smoke in studios and offices. I performed my tasks with diligence. After I was done shining them up, they were the cleanest ashtrays the station had ever seen.

I also used my time inside CKGM to practice announcing in empty studios and would sit with Earl as he did his show. With Earl's support, I volunteered at CKGM for more than a year.

Now, to get a job on the radio—an audition tape is needed. Earl took me into the studio one evening and produced the recording for me.

"Here's a newscast for you to read. It's from today. Then," Earl said, "you'll read the weather, I'll play a quick jingle, and you'll introduce the Andy Kim song, 'Baby I Love You,' which has a fourteen-second intro."

I had my very first "demo" tape. That's when I decided I needed a radio name. My real name—Jeffrey Ansel—didn't sound like any announcer I knew, so I tweaked it to flow smoother. I became "Jeff Ansell." Later in life, I had it legally changed.

Neither CKGM nor Radio Sir George paid me. In fact, I would have paid them if I'd had to—and believe me, I would have found the money.

High School Dropout...

On the first day of grade nine, my teacher asked my name. "Jeffrey Ansel," I said.

To which she replied, "Oh, you're the asshole."

What? Why did she call me that??

As a teacher, if she were to say that to a student today, it would be a page one above-the-fold story in the media. The teacher would be "canceled," to use today's parlance, vilified in social media, disciplined by regulators, and possibly lose her job.

Recently, I looked up the teacher on Facebook and wrote her, reminding her of what she'd said.

"Oh my, that was unacceptable. I apologize."

Maybe I had invited her anger—neither of us really remember. "No need to apologize," I said. "It's nice just to catch up with you."

I went to a pretty rough high school in Montreal. There was so much tension between Black and Jewish students that, more than once, my school found itself on the front page of the *Montreal Star* over racial skirmishes that took place.

One afternoon in the hallway, I was minding my own business when I was stabbed in the ass by Connie Johnson, then considered the so-called leader of the tough girls in school. She used a very sharp geometry compass to puncture my tuchus. It hurt.

I wasn't inclined to fight back because Connie would have kicked my ass and all other body parts, so this became the straw (or compass) that broke the camel's back, as it were.

I never went back to school. I never graduated.

I had been a scholarship student in high school, and when I quit I became a profound disappointment to my folks. It truly broke their hearts—especially my dad's.

The school wouldn't even let me attend the prom. It was embarrassing to be turned away, I must say, especially because I was with a date. We were all dressed up—with nowhere to go. As I recall, my date was cool about us being turned away because we ended up going to a really fancy restaurant.

Was I upset to have missed the prom, considered by many to be a personal milestone? No—I couldn't leave school fast enough. I was in too much of a hurry not to be a nothing.

Truth is—I wanted to quit school anyway so I could start pursuing my radio dream. I was in a hurry to get my life started. No one was going to do it for me, I realized early on.

Leaving school would give me the kick-start I was looking for.

Needing a Job...

The morning after the compass in the ass incident, I stayed in bed, with no need to get up for school.

At 7 a.m., my mother blew into my bedroom and yanked the covers back. "If you're not going to school, then get a job—today," she demanded. "You're not going to be a bum!"

So, I searched the wanted ads where I found an opening at a company called Atlantic Hosiery, which manufactured pantyhose.

Once I was accepted for the job, the foreman led me downstairs into a dark and musty basement. The ceiling was so low I had to crouch. There were a dozen people stashed in the basement—none of them looked at me. They were too busy hunched over their sewing machines making pantyhose.

My job was to take the two legs of the pantyhose and sew them together on a sewing machine with foot pedals that I had no clue how to use. I remember my grandmother had one, but it made no difference. I was too slow and couldn't ask for help because everyone was focused on their own machines. And besides, no one spoke English.

The hours were long, 7 a.m. to 6 p.m. We got paid by how much we produced, which meant a trip to the restroom or taking time to eat cost the workers money. No benefits either. The basement was hot, too—a literal sweatshop.

The pay was lousy—three cents a dozen, which was well below the legal minimum wage. I got paid $1.75 after working there for one whole day. Atlantic Hosiery needed to be held accountable for the way it violated laws designed to protect working people.

After that first day, I never went back to Atlantic Hosiery… until later.

My next job—albeit brief—was as a restaurant dishwasher. My boss docked my pay when I dropped a dish or a glass. That job didn't take either.

It was back to the wanted ads.

The next place I got a job was at Merit Clothing (remember the name). Merit manufactured men's suits, jackets, and pants. I was hired as a shipper. My job was to lift huge, heavy rolls of textile from the truck into the factory itself, where the trimmers would start cutting the fabric into suits.

Workdays at the clothing factory began early. My father would wake me about 6 a.m. Without saying a word, we'd go into our tiny kitchen and have a bite for breakfast, maybe a piece of toast and jam.

My father would then make his lunch and one for me, usually Kraft cheese and tomato. Putting our lunches into brown paper bags, he would turn and hand me my sandwich—all the while not saying a word.

He was so upset with my decision to leave school. I was supposed to be the educated one in the family. Yet there we were—a father and his teenage son who was supposed to be a professional—both going to work every day in the factories.

Leaving the house, we would walk uphill to the 160-bus stop, stand and wait, then board the bus together, all the while still not talking. From the bus, I would get off at my factory and he at his.

Creating a Path to Be More Than I Was...

When I began working at Merit Clothing, I committed to myself that every day on my lunch hour, I would work toward my goal of escaping the factory and getting onto the radio. I knew that if I planted the seed in my head and created a plan, I could fake it and make it happen despite my lack of inner confidence.

I needed to start somewhere, and for me, that meant to keep honing my broadcasting voice. However, if I started practicing without giving further thought to what steps might come after, I would have been flying blind, unsure of what to do, who to talk to, or where to go next.

So, I added more steps to my plan to get me where I needed to go. I broke my goal of being on the radio into four bite-sized, straightforward steps. If my end goal was to see myself on the radio, what did I need to do first to get there?

Step #1 Practice—Practice—Practice

The practice I was already doing, so I was covered on that front.

Step #2 Call one radio station each day begging for an audition

I had a thirty-minute lunch hour, which gave me an opportunity to make the calls, though there was little, if any, privacy.

Step #3 Do a great audition

I needed to show I had talent. As nervous as I would be in an actual audition, I knew I had to perform.

Step #4 Get a paying on-air radio job

I visualized myself on the air in a broadcast studio. In my head, it felt good. I was going to be on the radio—of that, there was no doubt.

To help me sharpen my focus even more, I discovered that breaking targets into four steps works backward, too. Sometimes even more effectively. It's a process I was inadvertently using long before I heard Steven Covey talk about the method.

In other words, by seeing the end in mind, the steps leading up to it can be even clearer. What is the end goal? Start there. Then, work your way back to where you need to start.

Step #4 Get a paying on-air radio job

Step #3 Do a great audition

Step #2 Call one radio station each day begging for an audition

Step #1 Practice—Practice—Practice

There were about ten English radio stations in the city. I would call one station a day, which meant that I would connect with each radio station every two weeks or so.

And I had chutzpah!

When I called each station, I would ask to speak to the owner or general manager. In those days, they actually put the call through. After several months of pestering, the owner of one station—CFMB in Montreal—finally said, "Alright! Fine! Come down here already. I'll meet you and give you an audition."

The owner's name was Casimir Stanczykowski. He said to me, "If I give you an audition, do you promise not to bother me anymore?"

"Yes, sir. I give you my word."

We scheduled the audition for the Monday following.

Now—what to wear to the audition became an issue. In a 2011 YouTube recording[3], I talked about that audition and the clothes I wore that day. I was bullshitting when I said I borrowed nice clothes from a friend because I was ashamed to admit the truth.

In his 2005 bestseller *On Bullshit*, philosopher Harry Frankfurt defines bullshit as persuasion without regard for the truth. The truth here doesn't make me look good.

The truth is, I wanted to appear presentable, so I looked to Merit to (unknowingly) provide me with nice clothes to wear to the audition.

The clothes they manufactured were stylish and pretty pricey—unaffordable to people like me. But there was a way for me to score Merit clothes at a heavily discounted, less-than-appropriate price.

You see, at Merit, no garment was allowed to leave the factory if it had a flaw—a tear in the pants, a hole in the jacket, and so on. Flawed clothes went into a special pile, and every Friday, employees could rifle through the discard pile and buy the clothes at a fraction of the cost.

By being the first to arrive in the morning, I was able to handpick the clothes I liked and then use scissors to slightly cut and damage the fabric before tossing them into the discard pile. I would then hide the clothes at the bottom of the pile to make it difficult for others to get to them before me.

I would then pull my mom's Cadbury move, only I'd be causing the damage myself.

I hope the statute of limitations on *suit theft* has long passed.

In recounting that story on YouTube, I realized what I had actually done was steal from Merit—but I was too ashamed to admit it.

So, instead of admitting to being a thief, I chose to lie for one hundred please, Alex.

> *Which reminds me, I got tossed out of a* Jeopardy! *audition—for cheating.*
>
> *My sister Dina and her husband Buzzie lived in Brooklyn, and I spent every summer there as a youngster and teen.*
>
> *Away from home, I got to hang out with Buzzie, who I looked to as an older brother. We both loved the TV game show* Jeopardy! *and when they announced auditions for the show, Buzz and I went into New York to try out.*
>
> *Not quite old enough to qualify, I said I was nineteen and they let me in.*
>
> *As part of the audition, we sat next to each other in what looked like school desks. The person running the tryouts at the front of the room would reveal the answer, and we had to privately write down the question to it.*

The questions were tough.

Not knowing how to answer most of them, I looked over to see what Buzz was writing down.

I was spotted peering over at Buzzie's page, and they told both of us to immediately leave for cheating.

CHAPTER THREE

I Lied My Way onto the Radio

Aside from family and close friends, there are probably, I'd say, five to six people who make a meaningful difference in an individual's life. Casimir Stanczykowski is near the top of that list for me.

Mr. Stanczykowski himself came out to greet me in the lobby the morning of my audition. At 6'8", Mr. Stanczykowski was a bear of a man—huge, strong, and handsome. He was a proud Polish Catholic who came to Canada as a war orphan.

Mr. Stanczykowski created a thirty-minute radio program for the Polish community, which led to the birth of a radio station that catered to the needs of immigrants to Canada. The station linked people who shared a language or mother tongue. As a multicultural radio station, CFMB was broadcasting in twenty-two languages at the time, with announcers and program hosts representing cultures across the globe.

For my audition, I was put into a production studio and given a newscast to read. I was so nervous that I was shaking. I thought I did a terrible job.

At the end of the audition, Mr. Stanczykowski looked a little strangely at me. "How old are you?" he asked.

I had just turned seventeen, but I wasn't going to tell him that. "I'm nineteen."

He looked skeptical. "What's your education?"

I couldn't tell him that I'd left grade ten and was working as a clothing shipper. "I'm going to Sir George Williams University," I lied.

"Sir George Williams? What do you study?" he wanted to know.

I was stumped. "Communications," I stammered.

"Okay, leave us your phone number," he said.

Again, I panicked. In those days, nobody had cell phones or answering machines. My parents worked. The only number I could leave was my factory number, but that would reveal I wasn't telling the truth. So, I left the phone number of a girlfriend I had at the time because her mother was home during the day.

The next day, I went back to work at the factory. About ten o'clock that morning—I'll always remember it like it was in slow motion—I was called to the phone at the factory.

It was my girlfriend's mother.

"The radio station called," she said. "They want you to start on Monday."

This was the first major experience in my life that showed me that when you plant a big goal in your head, your brain will often find a way to make it happen.

That Monday was a holiday, so everyone in the house was still in bed when my 4 a.m. alarm went off. Getting up quietly for my first day on the job, I made my lunch and walked up the hill to the bus.

My job was to read the morning news in English. On day one, much to my surprise, they gave me several newscasts to read live on-air. My heart was thumping, yet I didn't screw up.

There I was, Jeffrey Ansel—now Jeff Ansell—seventeen years old and reading the morning news on CFMB radio—for real!

Up to then, it truly was the proudest moment of my life.

When the air shift ended, I was eager to go home and find out if my parents had been listening. Sure enough, I walked into our tiny living room and saw my parents' radio from the bedroom (best radio in the house) placed in the center of the coffee table in the middle of the room.

Sitting around the coffee table were my mother, father, sister, aunt, and grandmother. They had all been listening to me on the radio.

Of all my memories, that one continues to be a keeper.

Each of us, I think, wants to be able to please our parents and to be able to show them that we made out okay. But particularly after the pain that my mom and dad had felt after I quit school, I was grateful that they could see my life, or at least career trajectory, was starting to point in the right direction.

I later went on to work at some of the biggest radio and TV stations in the country, but that first day on-air at CFMB was one of the sweetest moments of all.

One perk of having the CFMB job was being able to invest in a car with some help from my parents. Soon after taking ownership of an Orange Datsun ($2,800 new), I drove four hundred miles to Toronto, the country's largest radio market.

Reaching Toronto was like arriving in Mecca. I immediately drove to 1331 Yonge Street, the home of CHUM Radio, where famous news guys like Dick Smythe and celebrity DJs like Wolfman Jack were on the air.

I stood on the street outside the station and peered in through their big picture window in front, just like I had outside CKGM.

Seeing the microphones and recording equipment, watching the news people prepare the next broadcast—I began to dream. "I want this," I said to myself, re-affirming my commitment to get it.

But the timing wasn't right. I was not in the least bit ready for Toronto radio, both in terms of substance and style. Frankly, I needed to become a better announcer and news reporter.

Besides, Mr. Stanczykowski became like a second father to me. Before working at CFMB, I'd reported to a foreman who yelled: "Pick up that fabric! Take it off that truck! Hurry up—you're going too slow!" Now, I was being treated with dignity.

Mr. Stanczykowski trusted me and demonstrated it in so many ways—like having me read the morning news, one of the most important time slots on a radio station, that very first day.

He also took a special interest in my welfare and development. Just off the street, I didn't really have a clue what I was doing most of the time. Yet, he continually nurtured me. Concerned that I didn't have enough training and background, Mr. Stanczykowski hired a former actor and broadcaster whose only job was to mentor and teach me.

Mr. Stanczykowski helped me become a CFMB personality—the "voice of English" on this multi-lingual ethnic radio station. Within six months, at age seventeen, I became the country's youngest news director.

Always a classy dresser in a suit, tie, broadcloth shirt, and cufflinks, Mr. Stanczykowski looked and carried himself like a diplomat. Once, at a company party, Mr. Stanczykowski bent down to kiss the hand of my date that evening—European style. Not seeing the cigarette between her fingers, he kissed the burning ash and didn't flinch as he straightened himself out.

Mr. Stanczykowski was kind to me in the little things as well. He'd invite me into his office just to talk. Eventually, I ended up telling him my real age and the truth about my education, or lack of it. But by that point, it didn't matter.

Promoting the Jackson 5...

My air shift at CFMB began at 5 a.m. and I was done work by 12 p.m. My friends were all at school, so I had a lot of time on my hands with nothing to do.

My job at the radio station opened a lot of doors. It gave me instant credibility to walk into new situations simply by telling people where I worked.

One day, I heard a radio commercial promoting a Jackson 5 concert at the Autostade stadium in Montreal. I thought the commercial sucked, so I contacted the big boss of the company promoting the concert. His name was Malachi Throne.

"Hello, Mr. Throne—I'm Jeff Ansell of CFMB Radio. I heard the commercials you're airing to promote the Jackson 5 show, and I can produce better spots for you." (I had never produced a radio commercial before. I figured CFMB's production people would help.)

"I also have a few ideas about how to promote your show. Can I come and meet you?"

"C'mon over," he said.

Interestingly enough, their offices were literally three blocks from where I lived as opposed to being downtown or in a fancy area. I met with Malachi, who was from New York and was well above 6'6". He was interested in my ideas and brought me on board.

In addition to the Jackson 5, MD Productions' upcoming roster of concerts featured the Commodores (before Lionel Richie became famous on his own), Earth, Wind & Fire, the Temptations, the O'Jays, and Kool & the Gang.

Like the talent he booked for his concerts, Malachi was Black, making me the only white guy in the whole outfit.

I always suspected that Malachi figured that I had a natural flair for business because I was Jewish. I'm afraid that when those skills were being handed out way back when, I was hiding behind the door. Malachi was unaware that I knew sweet bugger all about business generally or promoting concerts specifically.

Still, as an outcome of that initial meeting, I started producing and voicing radio commercials for MD Productions. In my best and deepest radio voice, I would do a lead-in like, "MD Productions presents the Jackson 5 and the Commodores, Wednesday, August 29th at the Montreal Autostade."

Malachi liked me, and despite my young age (eighteen), he gave me increased responsibility at MD Productions, from promoting shows to making sure all the terms of their contracts were being respected.

A few hours before the Jackson 5 show, I discovered it was Michael Jackson's fifteenth birthday (August 29th, 1973), and we needed to acknowledge that in some way.

"Go buy Michael a birthday cake," Malachi told me. "Here are the keys to the company van."

I had never driven a van before, and I needed to get on the highway to find a bakery. I got in the van, drove to a large bakery (safely, I'm grateful to say), and picked out a chocolate cake. I had the counter person write "Happy Birthday Michael" on it. Little did she know who the cake was for.

Hopping in the van, I raced back to the concert venue, holding the cake in my lap so it wouldn't get jostled on the ride there.

About an hour before the show was scheduled to start, the Jacksons arrived at the stadium. I hadn't met the brothers, and I was a big Michael Jackson fan. Who wasn't?

They walked into the dressing room in ascending order of height, as if they were walking onto the stage. Michael led the way. It struck me as odd, so regimented and rigid.

What initially got my attention was how big their afros were and how their bell-bottom pants were large enough to store a basketball in.

Upon entering the dressing room, Michael broke away from the bunch and went off to a corner to sit by himself. The other brothers, Jermaine, Marlon, Jackie, and Tito settled on the other side of the room, laughing and joking, leaving their brother alone.

They were very friendly. I thought it strange, however, that Michael was off by himself. As tempted as I was to talk to Michael, I didn't want to intrude, in case being alone was part of his pre-concert ritual.

We cut up the cake and passed it around. The next moment, in came this man who had great presence. It was their larger-than-life father, Joseph, and he was holding the hand of his seven-year-old daughter, cute as a button with tiny pigtails. "I'd like you to meet my daughter, Janet," he said.

The brothers (except Michael—I didn't want to disturb him) autographed a paper plate for me, which lies in a box somewhere in our storage unit. (I keep threatening to look for it.) But I felt sorry for Michael, sitting off by himself, especially on his birthday.

Screwing Up with the Temptations…

Three days after the Jackson concert, we featured the Temptations with the O'Jays as the opening act. This time, I buggered up.

The plan was for the O'Jays to perform for an hour, and, after a break, the headliners would take the stage. I was in the dressing room with the Temptations when their road manager asked, "Where's the Hawaiian Punch?"

"Excuse me?" I responded.

"Our Hawaiian Punch—where is it?" repeated the road manager. Hawaiian Punch?

"Our contract has a rider obliging you, the promoter, to stock the dressing room with cans of Hawaiian Punch."

It was news to me. I must have missed that when reviewing the contract. I was later told that contracts with performers would often include riders, like that one about Hawaiian Punch, which served to determine whether the concert promoter studied the contract or not.

It was a Saturday night after 7 p.m. By this time of the evening, the grocery stores were closed. How was I supposed to get cans of Hawaiian Punch for the Temptations?

I panicked, feeling responsible for not carefully reviewing the contract and its riders. In a worst-case scenario, no Hawaiian Punch meant delays in getting the Temptations on stage, or worse yet—maybe they would refuse to perform.

Desperate for Hawaiian Punch, I called my sister Dina who was visiting Montreal for the concert. She hadn't yet left the house for the concert.

"Dina, I haven't got time to explain. Go through the cupboards and find me cans of Hawaiian Punch—and hurry." I said to her breathlessly. "It has to be Hawaiian Punch—nothing else will do. The concert depends on it!"

When the O'Jays finished their performance, crews were re-conforming the stage to get ready for the Temptations—and still no Hawaiian Punch. So, I got on stage and announced to the thousands in the audience, "Will the lady with the Hawaiian Punch please come to the stage."

Then, I spotted Dina hurrying down from the stands, carrying two large shopping bags containing the Hawaiian Punch. When she reached the stage, I grabbed the shopping bags and raced to the Temptations' dressing room. The show went on as planned.

As with my gigs on Radio Sir George and the volunteer work with Earl at CKGM, I never got paid for the work promoting concerts. And I didn't expect to—because that wasn't part of my deal.

Yet one more example of how I took a job for free, knowing there would ultimately be a payoff—even if it didn't involve dollars.

I realize not everyone can do that, these days especially, but working for free at times paid off handsomely for me.

Doors can open if and when motivation can go beyond dollars.

Disappointing Mr. Stanczykowski...

As I became more accomplished as an announcer at CFMB, I began receiving job offers from other radio stations in town.

Strangely, within fifteen minutes of every job offer I received, Mr. Stanczykowski would walk into the newsroom and tell me, "I'm giving you an extra $50 a week." That happened several times, always within moments of me being offered another job.

Even after I discovered that Mr. Stanczykowski was listening in on my phone conversations from the master switchboard at his giant desk, I didn't mind. I revered him that much.

That's one reason it hurt as much as it did when I quit CFMB after working there for a year. CKGM, the rock station my friends listened to, wanted to hire me as a news announcer. CKGM was where I'd taped record jackets and cleaned ashtrays thanks to "Live Earl Jive."

Even though CKGM didn't, as a rule, do investigative reporting, I would at least be roaming the streets of Montreal in search of news. At CKGM, I'd be an on-air news broadcaster *and* field reporter.

When I told Mr. Stanczykowski I was leaving CFMB, he became misty-eyed. "I just bought a radio station in Winnipeg and I want you to build a newsroom there," he told me.

I had to turn him down. He was deeply upset.

One of the qualities that impressed me about Casimir Stanczykowski was his generosity. He always noted my fascination with a painting on his wall. Seeing me looking at it one last time, he said, "Take the painting."

"I can't take that," I responded immediately.

"Take it!" he said once more.

"Sir, I can't take it."

"Okay," he said. "Then I insist you take this instead." From his desk, he picked up a piece of Polish handicraft and handed it to me. Small, round, and made of wood, it was designed to store mini mementos, like paper clips and small tchotchkes.

"When you become the president of your own radio station, you put that on your desk, and you remember me."

I never chose to follow in those footsteps, but to this day, I still have his gift of handicraft on my desk at home.

Polish handicraft

The way Casimir Stanczykowski died spoke to the way he lived. Long after I left the station, there was a company picnic. Mr. Stanczykowski got in his car to get ice cream for the kids. He was killed in a car accident on his way to the store.

Mr. Stanczykowski was a great man, and I miss him. I will forever be in his debt, for many reasons. He took a chance on a seventeen-year-old kid and changed the kid's life forever.

Working with Tony the Tiger...

At CKGM, one of the biggest perks was the use of the station cruiser to roam around town.

Remember, we had no car when I was a kid, so it was neat driving around the city in a car with "CKGM" written in big, brassy letters on both sides. In the evening, I even got to take the car home and park it on my street. It was a big thrill.

At CKGM, I was rubbing shoulders with some of the best voices in radio and the people I'd listened to as a kid. At times, I was so in awe of these personalities that I was afraid to start a conversation with them.

More important to my career, I had the opportunity to work for news director Lee Marshall, a big, booming guy from New York who had the deepest voice I had ever heard.

Lee was a big shot in the North American radio industry and a top voiceover artist. In fact, Lee was the voice of Tony the Tiger[4] and was the wrestling announcer for Ted Turner's World Championship Wrestling (WCW).

Former Los Angeles Dodgers manager Tommy Lasorda once said, "If G-d ever wanted to make a speech, Lee Marshall would get the call."

After working at CKGM for about a year, I graduated from weekend to afternoon news and occasionally filled in for Lee in the prime-time morning slot. As a reporter, I was assigned to cover all types of "spot" news happening in the city, from community events and fires to news conferences and police briefings. It was great "on the ground" experience.

My first-ever investigative report had particular meaning for me. The report highlighted how workers at Atlantic Hosiery were mistreated by the company. This was the factory I had very briefly worked at after quitting high school.

Workers at Atlantic Hosiery were grossly underpaid and toiled in unacceptable conditions. They were taken advantage of by greedy factory owners who broke labor laws and needed to be held accountable.

It felt good reporting that story. Really good.

CKGM was a valuable place to develop my craft. I became one of the main voices at the station, an accomplishment in itself since we had some very talented announcers.

However, for someone wanting to do the high-profile morning news, it also became a dead end because that was Lee Marshall's spot.

Since he wasn't going anywhere soon, it was time for me to start looking elsewhere for the next rung on my ladder.

Jeff on the radio

Pulling On-Air All-Nighters...

One morning, I received a phone call from George Ferguson, news director at CFCF.

This was the station I'd visited with my mom and my friends when I was twelve, and it was the radio station my mom and I listened to in the morning after my dad went to work. Plus, it was the TV station most everyone in town watched.

George offered me a job doing the overnight news on radio. It was a tough time slot, one that no one really relishes. But I took the position because this station had a large, bustling newsroom and was dedicated to quality news on both radio and TV. Instead of occasional newscasts as on other stations, CFCF radio had news every thirty minutes, twenty-four hours a day.

It just so happened that George also used to be the assistant news director at CHUM, one of the most popular rock stations in the country. "Stay with me, Jeff. I'll work with you, train you, and prepare you for Dick Smythe and CHUM," George told me. All young broadcasters wanted to work at CHUM, and George knew it.

So, for twelve months, I worked for George, reading the news on the overnight shift from 11 p.m. to 7 a.m. The overnight shift gets to you after a while, especially in the winter. You finish work before the sun comes up and sleep until after the sun goes down. Not seeing much of the sun for days at a time can wreak havoc with your spirits.

Despite assurances I'd been given that I would eventually get off overnights, it wasn't happening. "Give me another shift George or send me to CHUM."

But no change. So, I submitted my letter of resignation.

Friends of mine were about to travel across the continent, and I wanted to join them. I thanked George for all his help and left for my cross-country trek.

Words Come Back to Haunt...

After three months, returning home from my trip, I needed a job. That's when I discovered my local reputation had been in tatters while I was gone because of something foolish I said.

I had visited my friend Isaac Shane, the overnight DJ at CFOM Radio in Quebec City. At three in the morning, I begged Isaac, "Please let me on the air. Nobody's listening—let me introduce a couple of songs and maybe read a public service announcement or two."

Thinking no one from the station was up at that hour, Isaac let me sit in the big chair and DJ.

I don't know what I was thinking. I got on the air and said, "If you're horny, give me a call!" and I gave the station hotline number.

Wouldn't you know it—the phone immediately rang. It was the president of the station. "Who the hell are you, and what the hell are you doing on my radio station?" he thundered into the phone. "Get off the air now and never come back to my station or to Quebec City—ever!"

Fortunately, Isaac was allowed to keep his job.

Somehow, the Quebec City recording of me being an idiot made its way back to Montreal. So now, everyone in the radio business in town heard how I had made a fool of myself that night in Quebec City. My name was mud—deservedly so.

After the tape made the rounds, I applied for jobs at some of the city's biggest radio stations, and the only one that showed any interest in me was the smallest station in town. They offered me next to no money.

"Jeff, who else would hire you?" the news director said to me.

I knew it was time to literally get out of town.

Moving to the Bigtime...

Though I was pretty well black-balled in Montreal, I did receive several offers from top radio stations elsewhere in the country, including one from CFTR in Toronto, Canada's fastest-growing rock station, just below CHUM in popularity and ratings.

The first time CFTR approached me was actually more than a year earlier. Out of the blue one day, news director Robert Holiday called and offered me a job. That initial job offer flustered me so much that I immediately said no. I didn't think I was good enough yet to be on Toronto radio. Lack of confidence still plagued me.

Now, this time around—I was ready. CFTR sent me an airplane ticket (my first-ever flight) and had someone pick me up at the airport.

Robert Holiday was a short, stocky fellow and one of the most intimidating people I have ever met, not only in the broadcasting industry, but anywhere.

He regularly terrorized all the young reporters in his newsroom. When any one of us would miss a big story or screw up, he would swear up and down at us and say, "I'll kick your ass down Yonge Street!"

At CFTR, I worked evenings and weekends, sometimes on the road as a reporter but mostly on-air as a news announcer. One night, I was assigned to do the 8:30 p.m. and 11:30 p.m. news. After the first newscast, there wasn't much happening, so around nine o'clock, I put my feet on the news desk to watch the *Mary Tyler Moore Show* on TV.

Moments later, Bob walked in. "Turn that %&$#! thing off," he yelled. (Let's just say he used various, less complimentary words.) "When you work in this !#&@% newsroom, you find some &#%@#! news to report on."

He scared me so badly that I never again turned on the TV to pass the time while at work.

Celebrity Interviews...

At CFTR, I met a number of my favorite performers like Eugene Levy and musical artists, including Santana and Mike Love of the Beach Boys.

In the early seventies, I was a big fan of *Second City Television* (SCTV), the half-hour comedy show featuring skits, highlighting the talents of Eugene Levy, Catherine O'Hara, John Candy, and Rick Moranis, among others. Before he was on SCTV, Rick and I did the afternoon show together on CHUM FM for a while.

One Saturday morning, I was interviewing a young Eugene Levy, then in his late 20s. After our interview, Eugene and I went for breakfast to Bob's Big Boy on Yonge Street. Eugene lamented the state of his career, which he felt was going nowhere. Recently, Eugene won the Emmy Award for best actor for his TV series *Schitt's Creek,* which itself captured nine Emmys in one evening.

Being on the radio provided me with opportunities to interview very interesting people.

I once got word that the actor Mickey Rooney[5] was staying at Toronto's Sutton Place Hotel. Between ages fifteen and twenty-five, Mickey Rooney made forty-three films for MGM. When he was nineteen, he was the first teenager to be nominated for an Academy Award.

So, I called the hotel and asked for Mickey Rooney's room. Usually celebrities book into hotels using fake names so they won't be bothered, I guess, by people like me. I was surprised when they put me through.

As soon as he answered the phone, I recognized Rooney's distinctive voice. "Mr. Rooney, my name is Jeff Ansell of CFTR Radio. If you would be kind enough, I would like to do a short interview with you."

"I am not Mickey Rooney," snapped the man who answered the phone.

Baloney. It was Mickey Rooney.

"Sir, the interview will take about five minutes or so," I said.

"I told you—I am not Mickey Rooney!" he bellowed.

"Mr. Rooney, I just want to ask a few questions about your visit to Toronto."

"You've got the wrong guy."

Sensing he was about to hang up on me, I said, "Mr. Rooney, the tape is rolling."

"Hi, Toronto—it's great to be here," and so the interview began.

Just Because I Don't Believe It...

I was still overly fixated on how I sounded. Bob helped me understand that "the voice" is just a tiny part of who we are and what we do as broadcast reporters. He also made me realize that I truly was lazy at times, and that would cause me to miss important stories, or at the very least, the ones of interest.

Like the time I was tipped off about Margaret Trudeau partying with the Rolling Stones at a local nightclub. Margaret was much younger than her husband, Canadian Prime Minister Pierre Trudeau. She was a real true spirit—hippie-like. Margaret was a woman with a mind of her own and enjoyed a good time.

About 10 p.m. I received an anonymous phone call in the newsroom: "Margaret Trudeau is at the El Mocambo bar hanging out and partying with the Rolling Stones," the caller said. "They're smoking weed."

Yeah, yeah, sure, I thought. Another crank call. "Thanks a lot for calling. Goodbye." I hung up.

Margaret Trudeau was on the front page of a leading newspaper the next day. It was a story and photo of Margaret Trudeau smoking a joint, enjoying herself with the Rolling Stones. The paper even had a photo of her exposing her vachooch. I couldn't believe it.

A hot tip had been given right to me, and I'd completely ignored it. Okay—the story wasn't going to change the course of human history, but it was newsworthy.

That reminds me—when former network news anchor David Brinkley was asked, "What is news?" he responded, "News is what I say it is."

When Bob discovered that I missed the story, he chewed me out royally. "You dumb, lazy, &★$%#%★&$!" Taking it very personally, I licked my wounds for days.

In spite of his intimidating tactics, Bob Holiday taught me more about being a reporter than anyone else I met in my career. His guidance was badly needed.

"You know what your problem is, Ansell?" Bob asked me. "If a news story doesn't fit your past experience or have a reference point for you, you dismiss it."

Bob was bang-on.

"If it's a story that seems too hard for you to believe, you immediately assume it isn't true."

Bob taught me the importance of suspending disbelief and provided me with the tools and skills needed to find and report news. He taught me what questions to ask, how to ask them, what to listen for, what to focus on, and how to follow through.

It was a painful lesson, but again, one of the most important in my career. Just because I didn't believe something, did not mean it wasn't real or hadn't happened. Almost daily in the world of news, one is confronted with the outrageous, the absurd, and the "impossible."

However, what's absurd and outrageous is often possible.

That's what makes it news.

Styx and Stoned—a Powerful Setback...

You know the saying, "Man plans, G-d laughs." Life threw me a curveball during my second year at CFTR.

The month was January. I was twenty-one years old and hoping to move to Los Angeles to be on the radio. LA was a huge radio market, and only the best and most talented broadcasters were on-air there. I even bought an airline ticket and scheduled job interviews with top LA stations.

Then, along came Styx, a rock group famous for hits like "Come Sail Away," "Too Much Time on My Hands," "Mr. Roboto," and "Lady." Styx came into the radio station one evening to promote their show planned for the next night, which I was looking forward to.

When my interview with Styx was over, we were all hungry, so we went down to Caesar's, the steakhouse next door. We had a great meal, and then the group invited me back to their hotel to party.

There were so many of us in the hotel room that there were no chairs left, so I sat on the floor. Lead singer Dennis DeYoung, Tommy Shaw, and brothers Chuck and John Panozzo regaled us with stories of sharing the stage with the Kinks, David Bowie, and Rush, among others. There was a lot of beer, and we passed around several joints. I was with Styx and stoned.

I stayed till four in the morning.

After going home to sleep, I woke up late that afternoon to get ready for Styx's concert. I had a friend over who was joining me for the concert. Barefoot, wearing only jeans and no shirt, I went to the kitchen to prepare some food. The plan was for us to have hot dogs and French fries for dinner.

I put cooking oil in a pot and waited for the oil to heat up so I could throw the fries in. That's when my friend Renée called.

"Hey Renée, you'll never guess who I was partying with all night. Styx! Yeah, we went back to their hotel room. It was great, and tonight I'm going to their show."

I got so engrossed in my conversation with Renée, I forgot about the oil on the stove. Hearing a "swoosh" sound, I glanced into the kitchen and saw huge flames coming off the pot. Flames so high, they were tickling the ceiling.

I dropped the phone and ran into the kitchen, not having a clue what to do. I grabbed the pot of fire, ran to the front door of my sixteenth-floor apartment, and flung the door open.

"Fire, fire, fire!" I screamed as I ran up and down the hallway. I just wanted the burning pot out of my apartment!

But I couldn't let the fire spread to other apartments. Mrs. Lep, who lived directly next door, was blind. Not knowing where to go or what to do, I then ran back into my apartment foyer, still holding the burning pot with flames flying out of it.

"This can't be happening to me," I frantically thought to myself as I stood at the front door. "This only happens to other people."

Well, it was happening to me, and as soon as I accepted that fact, the handle of the burning pot melted and fell onto my bare feet. The carpet beneath me was on fire.

I smelled my flesh burning. It was painful. The fire had burnt up the sole of my left foot. Charred flesh was peeling off the bottom.

It was bad enough that I was hurt, but I couldn't let anyone else be hurt too—or heaven forbid, worse. I was thinking, of course, about my friend hiding in another room. I worried too for Mrs. Lep.

"Quick!" I yelled as loud as I could. "Throw me a blanket!"

My friend did—but the instant I put it over the flames, the blanket disintegrated. "Bring me another blanket!" I shrieked. I threw the second blanket onto the fire, and this time—it worked. The second blanket put the fire out.

My friend was okay. So was Mrs. Lep.

Once I could safely do so, I made my way back to the hallway and collapsed onto the ground as I heard fire trucks and ambulances outside.

For the first time since the burning pot fell on my foot, I allowed myself to feel the pain. It was excruciating. I'm told that's when my eyes rolled to the back of my head and I went into shock. I later discovered that I suffered first, second, and third-degree burns.

When the firefighters arrived and saw I was badly burned, they put me in the bathtub to cool my body while they quelled remnants of the blaze. Then, the paramedics put me on a stretcher and wheeled me out.

As we were leaving, I remember glancing through the large bank of windows in my living room. Looking out over the skyline, as I was being wheeled out on a stretcher, I had two thoughts.

My initial thought was, I should be the one standing a few feet away watching, but I'm the one on the stretcher in the reflection. There's got to be a mistake! I was the guy who reported on fires for five years, who stood outside burning buildings watching accident victims being carted away, then asking victims and family members, "How does it feel?"

My second thought was, I don't want this to be reported on the radio. I could only imagine hearing CFTR report the story...

"CFTR's Jeff Ansell was seriously burned in an apartment fire today. According to authorities, Ansell forgot he was cooking French fries when the pot of oil burst into flames on the stove. Panicking, Ansell ran up and down his sixteenth-floor hallway yelling "Fire." Miraculously, he was the only one hurt. Reports indicate Ansell had been smoking marijuana and drinking all night with the rock group Styx." That last part was my twisted mind at work

After coming home from the hospital burn unit, I spent three months in bed, recovering. Burns hurt like a son of a bitch.

Not wanting to worry my parents who lived in another city, I only told them about the fire when I was close to being healed. And even then, I played it down. If they knew I was hurt, they would have taken time off work, and I didn't want them to do that.

I still wanted to go to LA to be on the radio, but because my employer had paid me for the ninety days I was off work, I couldn't up and leave. I returned my plane ticket and canceled my LA interviews.

Staying on the job was the right thing to do, given CFTR's kindness during my recovery. When I eventually returned to work, the first story I reported on was fire safety in the home.

Oh yes—needless to say, I never made it to the Styx concert that night.

On-Air Panic Attack!...

Up to this point in my career, my focus had been mostly on "making it"—reaching my goal of working at CHUM.

Dick Smythe of CHUM pursued me to work on his station, but I had to turn Dick down because CFTR had taken such great care of me after the fire. I returned to the air in March and worked at CFTR for six more months before I felt it was okay to move on—to CHUM Radio.

I hadn't quite met my goal of being on CHUM by the age of twenty (I was twenty-one), but I had still accomplished my decade-long dream. I was now working in the CHUM newsroom. I went from peering in the window from the outside to looking out the window from the inside.

Essential to my working at CHUM was having the so-called CHUM sound. Despite what Bob Holiday had taught me earlier, I was still too fixated on how my voice sounded than on what came out of it.

Now, I needed to have the so-called CHUM sound. Some days, I'd drive to work and just before I'd arrive at the radio station for my shift, I would talk out loud in the car and think, how's my voice today? Is there timbre in it? Does it have range?

There were two other key aspects to my new job at CHUM. Aside from having the opportunity to do investigative reports and many interviews, I also prepared and delivered morning news on the hour.

That's when it happened to me for the first time. I had a panic attack live on the air on the country's biggest radio station.

While reading the 8:30 a.m. news, I realized shortly after I began that I did not have enough news to fill my seven-minute slot.

So, during a forty-five-second break while I played an audio news report from overseas, I jumped up from the studio chair, wildly swung open the door, raced sixty feet down the hallway, made a sharp left, then a quick right, and crashed through the newsroom door.

I grabbed some news copy without even looking at it (thankfully, it wasn't the pork belly futures report) and re-traced my route as I ran back into the news studio as fast as I possibly could.

I flung the studio door open, hurled myself onto the studio chair, threw on my headphones, flicked on my microphone, opened my mouth to read the news copy—and couldn't utter a word.

I had been running so fast that I had no breath left.

The headphones turn up the volume of what's going out on the air for the announcer to monitor. All I heard was me gasping for breath on the air as hundreds of thousands of people listened in.

What was initially a problem of breathing transformed into a panic attack. In my body, it was like the theme music from the movie *Jaws* had come alive. The shark was after me—boom-boom, boom-boom, boom-boom.

My heart started to race like a jackrabbit; I was sweating, light-headed, and shaking like a leaf. I was being eaten by the shark.

A tingling sensation started in my toes and moved its way up through my legs and my waist. I couldn't breathe. Then, the shark was in my throat and I couldn't swallow. My heartbeat got faster. As the shark reached my neck, my temples began to throb, and I could barely focus.

I remember the DJs in the next studio looking through the glass between us to see if I was alive.

Somehow, I finally managed to say something.

"In other news," I said, stammering, "the US Senate votes today (pause—trying to breathe) following the vote by the (nervous swallow) House of Representatives..."

Then, for three long minutes, I struggled to reach the finish line. The newscast ended, and music came through the headphones.

"Are you okay?" one of the announcers called to me off-air.

"I don't know," I answered truthfully. "I'm not sure what just happened. I've never had that happen before."

It took me ten minutes to leave the studio. Number one—I was in shock and deeply upset. Number two—I was very embarrassed.

A few days later, I was in the studio again, pondering what had happened that morning with the shark. Just the thought of it triggered another on-air panic attack. The shark kept on coming for me—boom-boom, boom-boom, boom-boom. The idea that I might have a panic attack every time I went on the radio was a horrible, overwhelming thought. I developed a fear of going on the radio.

That was the ultimate irony. I spoke for a living. Now, I was afraid to speak.

Very often in this world, rightly or wrongly, we (especially men) use our work to gauge our self-worth. I definitely did.

Not only was I now facing the daily threat of a panic attack, but my sense of worth and identity as a broadcaster also began to suffer—and that impacted the entire quality of my life. That's how deep I was at the time, I guess.

My live, on-air panic attacks were happening with greater frequency. They got so bad I thought I would have to leave the broadcasting business and go back to working in a clothing factory.

Regardless, I knew I had to find a way out of my anxious headspace.

In the weeks that followed, the attacks happened several more times. All I had to do was think about a panic attack and my heart would begin thumping. It didn't always happen every time I was on-air—but often enough.

I went to doctors and psychiatrists—nothing worked. I would even have tried Voodoo—that's how desperate I was.

To get my mind off my panic attacks, I would write down famous sayings, place them on the anchor desk, and look at them when I felt an on-air attack coming. Pithy little phrases to help me re-focus, like "Nothing human is alien to me." Those words must have meant something to me then, but I honestly don't know what. I laugh about it now, but it actually helped me avoid the panic attacks for a few days.

I later discovered it happened to other CHUM broadcasters. We all came to call it the CHUM ghost.

I loved working at CHUM Radio, despite my panic attacks. When I left the station after five years to go to CITY-TV, colleagues gathered to see me off.

In saying goodbye, I told them the story ". . . about a young boy who had a dream of working at CHUM. Late at night, the boy would listen to CHUM on his parents' radio and picture himself one day being on the air at the country's greatest radio station. On behalf of that young boy, I want to thank you for helping make his dream come true."

One Hot Night...

It was the hottest summer we had in years. Even the overnights were sweltering. People with no air conditioning slept on their balconies— hoping for a breeze, even a slight one.

I was still working at CHUM, sitting at my desk at 4:30 a.m. preparing for my final morning newscasts. There were only two of us in the building at that hour—me and the all-night disc jockey. He and I were talking in the newsroom when two young, attractive, blonde women stood at the CHUM window—the exact one I used to peer into years before.

They knocked on the window mouthing the words, "Let us in." We did and ushered them into the newsroom. They were each wearing long, summery dresses to cope with the scorcher.

That's when they quite unexpectedly lifted their dresses above their heads, exposing their nakedness. I looked at my colleague. He looked at me. We could not believe what we were seeing.

As interesting as it could have been he and I were highly unnerved. And besides, we had jobs to do.

By the way, the overnight DJ was John Roberts, now a host of *America Reports* on FOX News and formerly chief White House correspondent for the network.

On-TV...

That summer, I attended a talk by Elie Wiesel, a Holocaust survivor who, in fact, was the first to use the term *Holocaust* in the context of the Jewish slaughter.

The evening of Mr. Wiesel's speech, I found myself seated next to Moses Znaimer, the innovative founder of CITY-TV Toronto. Moses and I began chatting, and by evening's end, he offered me a job as a news producer at CITY.

My passion was to work as an investigative reporter and perhaps as a news anchor as well at some point in the future. But if getting in the newsroom door meant starting off as a producer, then I would do it. I didn't know, however, what the job of a producer was.

"Moses, let me shadow one of your producers for a day, and then I'll let you know whether I can do the job." He said yes.

After spending a day with the 6 p.m. news producer, I saw how nerve-wracking the job was. I just watched and stressed out. That day I had my first cigarette in five years!

The producer is the newsroom figurehead who assigns stories to reporters, sends camera people on shoots, decides the order of the stories, calls the shots from the studio control room during the broadcast, and (aside from the news director) is the big boss in charge of the 6 p.m. news.

Producing the news is a big job. For someone with no TV experience (me) to take on such a big job in a new medium was not only overwhelming but also intimidating. Plus, the other reporters, writers, editors, and assignment people would all know I was a novice, adding to the pressure. That alone would have me second-guessing myself with every move I made.

Besides, being a producer wasn't the job I wanted. Fortunately for me, a reporter's job opened up immediately after that, so three days later, I joined CITY-TV as an on-air reporter.[6]

In addition to my regular reporting duties, I also conducted long-form investigations, and soon after, I became a news anchor.

Make Others Look Good...

When CITY-TV launched weekend newscasts, I was tapped to co-anchor the 6 p.m. and 11 p.m. news with Anne Mroczkowski, a colleague I barely knew.

I was nervous. As cool as she was, I figured Anne must be nervous too. After all, we had never been on the air together anchoring the news.

So, the first time we went on air together, I told Anne beforehand, "I will bend over backward to make you look as good as possible on-air, and I ask you to do the same—make me look as good as possible on-air."

"Deal," Ann said.

We successfully co-anchored the news for a number of years.

By the way—if you recall, I asked you earlier to remember the name Merit Clothing, the factory I worked at and where I used to purposely damage pants and jackets so I could buy them at a really deep discount.

When I became a news anchor on TV, my wardrobe was now being provided by—you guessed it—Merit Clothing.

Anne Mroczkowski & Jeff

Live TV Panic Attack!...

One step forward, two steps back. The shark returned, coming back as angry as ever.

CITY-TV had a short, live broadcast prior to 6 p.m. to promote the upcoming newscast. It was called the *CITY Pulse News Flash*, and it came on during a break in the *Price is Right* game show.

The producer would ask whichever reporter was available to go on-air to read the *CITY Pulse News Flash*, which was about three minutes long. *News Flash* was live on-air directly from the newsroom, which meant that whoever was delivering it was surrounded by dozens of people who went silent once the camera turned on.

"Jeff, go handle *News Flash*," my producer said to me one afternoon.

Forget about the hundreds of thousands watching at home; as soon as I settled into position for the broadcast, I felt extremely self-conscious because everyone in the newsroom was looking at me. The people around me were freaking me out, triggering my panic.

As soon as the broadcast began, I felt the shark grab me—in front of everyone. I was having my first panic attack on live TV. I started to shake. My voice quivered. I couldn't breathe.

Half the people in the newsroom were looking at me in disbelief, and the other half were looking away, uncomfortable watching a train wreck unfold in real-time. I was humiliated.

Funnily enough—no one ever talked about it with me.

I dreaded going live on-air for fear I would have yet another meltdown in front of hundreds of thousands of people. From that point on, I was so afraid the producer would ask me to go on-air at five to read *News Flash* that every afternoon at 4:50 p.m. I would disappear from the newsroom and hide in a bathroom stall until 5:05. I would come out of the bathroom only when I knew *News Flash* was over.

I never knew if anyone ever noticed how I would mysteriously disappear just before *News Flash*. If so, now they know why.

CHAPTER FOUR

Confronting Jew-Haters and Hunting Nazis

Anti-Semitism wasn't really on my personal radar screen until an ugly confrontation at the McDonald's in Montreal, where my teenage friends and I hung out.

We were eating our burgers when this elderly couple walked in and headed to the counter. They were familiar faces in the neighborhood, and I frequently saw them at this McDonald's. They walked up to the counter to each order a coffee when suddenly, the door to the restaurant kicked open and in stormed this loud-mouth in his mid-twenties who yelled at the couple.

"You took my parking spot!" he shouted at the old man. "You are fucking Jews. Hitler should have killed you all!"

I couldn't believe what I was hearing. Never before had I heard anyone make such hateful comments—at least, not in person.

This Jew-hater threatened these two older people who simply wanted to mind their own business and enjoy a coffee. No one else in the restaurant seemed to move. Everyone was frozen on the spot, almost in a state of disbelief, as to what we were witnessing.

What happened next is right out of a dream.

I remember being overwhelmed with an anger unlike any other I had ever experienced. I went into a trance and had an out-of-body experience.

I saw myself get up from my seat, walk over to this Jew-hating punk, grab him by the shirt collar, lift him off the ground, and shake him vigorously while loudly repeating, "Don't you ever say that again!" The next thing I knew, police were pulling me off the jerk and I was jolted back into the moment.

Another time, when a woman called me a dirty Jew (again in a burger joint—what gives?) I literally spit in her face. Not terribly proud of that because my family was with me, but it seemed like the appropriate response at that moment.

At one radio station, the news director used to Jew-bait me with anti-Semitic comments he would make in the newsroom. I kept my mouth shut, believing he would embarrass himself in front of everyone. He kept doing it—over a period of several instances. Still, I didn't say a word.

Then one day, a young female intern came to work in the newsroom and the news director delivered anti-Semitic comments to her. It was bad enough that he taunted me, but to go after a young intern was too much. I went ballistic.

Later, he apologized to me, extending his hand.

I refused to shake it. I was wrong. A day or so after, I apologized to him for not accepting his apology and handshake, and then we got along fine.

My real battle with Jew-haters was to take on a new form in the months to come.

Ernst Zündel...

The first time I met Ernst Zündel, I literally picked him up by his jacket and threw him out of the CHUM building, tossing him onto Yonge Street. Here's why.

In 1978, NBC aired the mini-TV series *Holocaust*, based on the Gerald Green book. The series introduced the terrible events involving the slaughter of Jews at the hands of the Nazis.

So, when I received a news release from a group called the Concerned Parents of German Descent, I took notice. The group argued that today's Germans were being punished for the sins of a previous generation.

I felt it was a legitimate news story. The spokesperson for this group was a local graphic artist named Ernst Zündel. It was the first time I heard of him.

I invited Zündel to be interviewed on CHUM's *In Toronto* public affairs program, a daily sixty-minute show featuring interviews with authors, actors, politicians, and people in the news.

In Toronto provided a platform to cover every topic imaginable, including my numerous investigations to follow. Over the course of five years, I interviewed well over a thousand people for the *In Toronto* program.

For the first portion of the interview with Zündel, we discussed the impact of the *Holocaust* mini-series on the German community. But when the subject turned to the persecution of the Jews, Zündel referred to the "myth" of the Holocaust.

Not sure if I heard him properly, I asked Zündel to repeat what he said. Sure enough, I heard him right. "The Holocaust was a hoax," Zündel stated. He was a Holocaust denier! That's when I threw him out on his ass.

Ernst Zündel and I were to cross paths many times over the years.

Wikipedia describes Zündel as a pamphleteer, jailed several times in Canada for publishing literature "likely to incite hatred against an identifiable group."[7] His profile and influence grew over the years, especially after he published *Did Six Million Really Die?*

According to Zündel, "Out of the rubble for a nation laid waste by the Jews, the Fuehrer built an orderly, corruption-free, economically vibrant, and morally-pure society in which our men were manly." He describes Hitler as "a type of risen German Christ, a faith figure in the eyes of his people."[8]

Needless to say, Zündel was in the news a fair bit because of his trials and tribulations. At each court appearance in Toronto, Zündel and his mean-spirited evil cohorts would don construction helmets, spreading their hate on the way into the courthouse.[9] Later, in 1994, Zündel campaigned to ban the movie *Schindler's List* as "hate speech."

The US also went after Zündel on charges of being a threat to national security for overstaying his visa. Even Germany went after Zündel for inciting racial hatred.

The exterior of Zündel's home on Carlton Street in Toronto was surrounded by barbed wire. The inside of the home itself resembled a bunker and was home to other neo-Nazi misfits who slept in bunk beds and cots spread throughout the house.

As an investigative reporter, I admit that more than once I employed devious methods to ensure Zündel came across as a crackpot. When I did TV interviews with Zündel in his bunker, I would sometimes not give him a microphone to speak into so his voice would sound tinny. On occasion, I would also tell the cameraperson not to turn on the camera light so Zündel would come across as a madman spouting hate from a distance in the dark.

To me, Zündel was simply a despicable human being. But one thing's for sure, the son of a bitch knew how to get media coverage.[10]

At CITY-TV, the powers that be made me the designated reporter for the Jewish beat. I believe that being known as the "Jewish" reporter made me less appealing to other news media outlets and did impact my TV reporting career. In truth though, I took this role largely upon myself.

As much as I detested Zündel, I insisted on being the newsroom reporter who covered him. My fear was one of my less-read colleagues would actually provide a credible platform for Zündel to propagate his Jew hatred. I was concerned about Zündel-type stories being reported by people who had never read a history book and were naively susceptible to believing nonsense. "Really? You mean six million didn't die?? I never thought about it from your perspective."

Afraid that my colleagues might present historical revisionism as "news," I jumped in ahead to make sure it didn't happen—on my watch anyway. I developed that concern after a conversation with a fellow reporter.

"I just had a taxi ride with a cabbie who told me he doubted the Holocaust was for real."

"How did you respond to that?" I pressed.

"Well, the cabbie did make some interesting points," he responded.

I told him, "The next time you hear someone spout nonsense denying the Holocaust, tell the person, 'You're right, and Blacks were never slaves.'"

The last time I saw Zündel was when we bumped into each other in a downtown Toronto restaurant. He had just been ordered to be deported to Germany and was having a goodbye lunch with about a dozen of his Hitler-loving buddies. I was planning to ignore him, but he saw me and came over.

"Happy Rosh Hashanah (Jewish New Year)," Zündel said to me, extending his hand to shake mine. I refused to have physical contact with him—he was vermin.

"Ernst, you know I can't touch you," I told him.

That was the last we saw of each other.

Former *Toronto Sun* reporter Mark Bonokoski had similar sentiments about Zündel. "When Zündel was eventually released from that German prison, he complained his cell was no better than a 'chicken coop,'" wrote Bonokoski. "Compared to the concentration camps where six million Jews lived and died, however, it was a five-star hotel."[11]

Hunting Nazi War Criminals...

Sadly, the hate spewed by people like Zündel continues to grow.

After the Second World War, Canada opened its doors to admit 40,000 Holocaust survivors. Those prisoners who survived the horrors of the camps weren't the only Europeans allowed entry after the war. In fact, it was easier for Nazi war criminals and collaborators to gain entry into Canada after the war than it was for Holocaust survivors.

In the late seventies, I interviewed Simon Wiesenthal, the famed Vienna-based Nazi hunter. Mr. Wiesenthal was a Jewish Austrian Holocaust survivor, and following the war, he pursued justice by capturing Nazi war criminals.

My interview with Mr. Wiesenthal was conducted over the phone because he refused to come to Canada.

"I feel so bitter that Canada has a few hundred people, maybe even more, who committed war crimes," Mr. Wiesenthal told me. "The typical Nazi in Canada lives free for many years. No one knows his past, and his neighbors think he's a nice old man."

Mr. Wiesenthal was right.[12]

From the depths of my ignorance, I said to Mr. Wiesenthal, "Come on, I don't believe Nazi war criminals and collaborators are here. Give me the name of one Nazi war criminal or collaborator living in Canada," I pressed.

"Get the book *Wanted! The Search for Nazis in America*, by *New York Times* reporter Howard Blum," Mr. Wiesenthal told me. "Turn to page 214."

I did as Mr. Wiesenthal instructed.

Page 214 of Blum's book documented the crimes of Haralds Puntulis, a captain in the Aizsargi, representing the Nazi-supported Latvian Army. Puntulis was said to be responsible for the execution of 5,128 Jews and 311 Gypsies, and of sending more than 5,000 non-Jews to serve as slave labor in Germany. He was convicted in absentia by a Soviet court, which sentenced him to be shot to death.

The book said Puntulis' whereabouts were unknown. I found Puntulis in the Toronto suburb of Willowdale, a neighborhood replete with a strong Jewish community, ironically enough. Or was it? Many Nazi war criminals fleeing justice found a home amongst Jews, especially in Toronto.

Imre Finta, one Nazi in the Hungarian death machine, lived smack dab in the center of a strong Jewish Orthodox community. Finta was the owner of the popular Toronto restaurant Moulin Rouge, whose walls featured photos of Finta with well-known Jewish patrons.

What his customers did not know was that Finta had been a captain in the pro-Nazi Royal Hungarian Gendarmerie. In 1948, he was found guilty of war crimes in absentia by a Hungarian People's Court. He was convicted of kidnapping and forcibly confining 8,617 Jews prior to loading them into boxcars for deportation to Auschwitz.

Years later, Finta was put on trial in Canada before a jury in Ontario Supreme Court on charges of kidnapping, manslaughter, and robbery. To defend him, Finta hired lawyer Douglas Christie, whose specialty was defending anti-Semites.

Christie argued that Finta was simply following orders, adding that Jews were indeed a menace to security in 1944 when the Soviet army was advancing on Hungary. He argued that when Finta stole jewelry and other valuables from Jews, he was merely acting as a "tax collector." The jury of eight women and four men found Finta not guilty.

When I confronted Finta at his home, I waited outside while his German Shepherd barked menacingly at me through the front door. Finta told me repeatedly about his affinity for the Jews. "I have a Jewish doctor, I have a Jewish lawyer, I have a Jewish accountant, I love the Jewish people," he smugly said.

As an aging east European with an accent, Finta fit in well in the kosher restaurants and Jewish delis where no one suspected he was a murderer.

Haralds Puntulis fit in well, too—especially as the kind, gentle neighbor with the beautiful lawn and prized stamp collection. Puntulis' garden was beautiful, with bright orange, mauve, and white flowers growing around his house.

But it was an incongruous beauty, a beauty I couldn't reconcile with the pictures in my head of all those he had killed. It didn't seem just that this man should have spent the last thirty-four years living the good life while his victims lay buried in unmarked graves and ditches.

I hated every minute I worked on the Nazi investigation—because with each new piece of evidence that I gathered on Puntulis, I wanted to do him grievous harm.

I contacted Puntulis. He was a man of few words. "It's a very, very old case, and I'd rather not comment," he told me.

"Are you the Haralds Puntulis sentenced to death in Latvia?" I asked.

"Yes, that is so," he answered.

"Did you commit war crimes during World War Two?"

"No," he responded quickly.

"Should people forget about these crimes?"

A pause. "I actually don't know. I'd rather not comment on these things… I am reaching a very old age, and I wouldn't be bothered," he said.

A part of me was surprised Puntulis had admitted to his war crimes conviction. I'd expected him to deny it. From his perspective, why open the floodgates to further scrutiny and rock the boat now? After all, Canada had provided Puntulis and his wife Anna with a nice life.

Why would he publicly risk jeopardizing his status by acknowledging he was the Nazi I was searching for? Was it that Puntulis thought he was invincible—beyond legal and judicial reproach? Did he think no one would care if he admitted to his past?

Maybe he figured that at his age, what's the point of lying anymore? Or maybe he was just tired of carrying the burden of guilt all these years. Doubtful, but possible, I suppose.

But his answer to the question of whether he was the Haralds Puntulis convicted of war crimes was all I needed for now.

As part of my investigation, I managed to obtain Puntulis' Gestapo pass and matched the birth date with his driver's license.

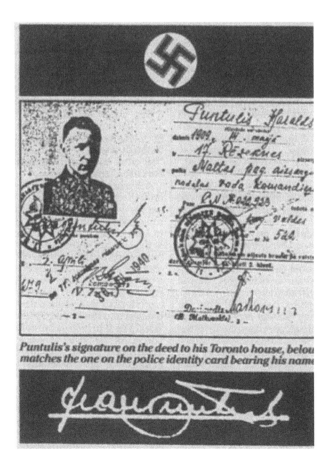

Puntulis' Gestapo pass

Matching his signature with his mortgage, I knew conclusively that it was him. Beyond any doubt, I had proved he was indeed the one and only Haralds Puntulis.

Then, in order to prove he was a killer, I began researching his life, tracing every step he took from 1939 onward. Puntulis had come to Canada on the CP *Empress,* docking in Quebec City before he made his way to Toronto to work as a contractor.

To learn what it was like living next door to a killer, I spoke with several of Puntulis' neighbors—one of whom told me that it's time for "everybody to forget about the Second World War and go on."

That sentiment was widespread among Puntulis' neighbors whom I spoke to. Despite overwhelming evidence proving his guilt, Puntulis claimed to have been hiding in the forest during the war.

Puntulis' wife Anna was quoted telling a neighbor, "Do you really think I could live with a man that has done what Harry is accused of? I was with him through it, and he's never been involved in any of this."

I went to the federal government to push them to take action against Puntulis. No dice.

Neither the Canadian government nor the RCMP (Royal Canadian Mounted Police) was interested in going after Nazi war criminals and their all too willing murderous helpers. At the time, the Canadian government leaders were Prime Minister Pierre Trudeau and Jean Chrétien, his then-minister of justice and future Canadian PM.

The Liberal government of the day did not want to upset East Europeans across Canada, who would see the prosecution of Puntulis as a provocative act against their community.

Politicians do like getting re-elected, after all.

Frustrated by the lack of help I was getting from the Canadian government, my investigation turned southward.

The US Government Feeds
Me Secret Info...

The US Justice Department in Washington DC created the Office of Special Investigations (OSI), run by Allan Ryan. OSI's mandate was to find and expel from the United States all Nazi war criminals and collaborators who had become naturalized American citizens.

Every week for three months I called Allan Ryan, just about begging him to grant me access to Justice Department files on Puntulis and other Nazi war criminals in Canada. The Americans maintained meticulous records on the matter.

Believe it or not, the Soviets also kept highly detailed records and provided a credible source of information in my investigation with many eyewitness and survivor accounts.

As for Ryan, he repeatedly refused to allow me access to his files on Puntulis or anyone else.

He kept telling me that the RCMP should be requesting the files and evidence, but they weren't, and he was not about to hand sensitive government documents to a reporter.

I persisted, and finally, in what must have been my tenth call— Ryan said yes. "Be at my office on K Street tomorrow morning at eight," Ryan said to my surprise.

Ryan was clearly pissed off with the lack of action on Canada's part. "I'll give you access to the Puntulis files and let you review survivor and eyewitness depositions and video accounts," Ryan told me.

I flew to Washington DC that evening. Early the next morning, I met with Allan Ryan, who in later years went on to write *Quiet Neighbors: Prosecuting Nazi War Criminals in America* and was a historical advisor on *Elusive Justice: The Search for Nazi War Criminals.*

Ryan set me up with my host for the day, OSI criminal investigator and lawyer Bert Falbaum. Bert was responsible for conducting investigative efforts to detect and bring to justice the alleged Nazi war criminals residing in the United States. He'd coordinate with his counterparts in national and international law enforcement and intelligence communities.

Canada refused to play ball.

Bert made files, videos, and all other Puntulis-related documents available to me. Over the course of my DC visit to the Justice
Department, I pored over hundreds of pages of documents and hours
of video-recorded testimony identifying Puntulis as the leader of his
regional killing machine.

I will never forget one document I read in particular—it squeezed
me by the guts and would not let go. The document told of how
Puntulis ordered one of his officers to pull the trigger on an eleven-
year-old boy. He did, but the boy wasn't killed. The officer had flubbed
the shooting. The boy was still alive. So, Puntulis grabbed the gun and
shot the boy himself, killing him.

When I read that, I started to shake. "I'm going to kill Puntulis," I
told myself.

As crazy as that might sound, at the time, it made perfect sense
to me. I would kill this son of a bitch murderer on behalf of his
thousands of victims—including the eleven-year-old boy whose fate
struck deeply in my heart.

A New Nazi Emerges...

After studying evidence from survivors and witnesses in the
Washington offices of the justice department, I gathered the files in
my briefcase and went to thank Bert, the OSI lawyer who'd assisted
me throughout the day. He, along with Allan Ryan, had been a tremendous help in my quest for justice back home in Canada.

Then, what happened next is straight out of the movies.

That evening, a Friday, as I was about to leave his office and head to
Dulles Airport—Bert reached into his desk, pulled out a large brown
paper envelope, and tossed it on his desk toward me. Then, he wheeled
his chair around so his back was to me as he faced the window.

He clearly saw my reflection in the window and the perplexed
look on my face. It took me a moment to realize he wanted me
to take the envelope without watching me do it—directly anyway. I
grabbed the envelope and shoved it into my briefcase. Bert swiveled
his chair back around to face me.

It turned out that the contents of that envelope would change history.

In my cab en route to Dulles, I remember driving in front of the White House as I pulled out the envelope Bert gave me. (Pre 9/11, Pennsylvania Avenue was open to vehicles.)

Inside the envelope was a photograph of Helmut Albert Rauca.[13] He was the top SS person in Kaunas, Lithuania, and was responsible for killing thousands of Lithuanian Jews.

Helmut Rauca

My father's father was from Lithuania, though my grandfather thankfully emigrated to Canada before World War One.

Helmut Rauca was the "Jewish specialist" in the local German administration. His mandate was clearly spelled out—he was in charge of executing Hitler's plan to exterminate Jews in his region and to provide slave labor for the civilian authorities. Rauca himself personally picked who to kill and often carried out the deed himself.

The blood of innocent Jews literally dripped from his hands.

A Rauca Survivor...

Faigie Schmidt Libman was seven years old and living in Kaunas when Germany Invaded Lithuania. The year was 1941. The month was October.

"I was born Feiga Schmidt in Kaunas (Kovno), Lithuania, in 1934. I was an only child," recalls Faigie in an interview.[14]

"We were ordered to assemble at Democracy Square, where Helmut Rauca, the SS master sergeant of the ghetto, divided families right and left. Those on the wrong side were sent up to the Ninth Fort and machine-gunned over open pits that became mass graves."

Hiding her yellow star of David, Faigie's mother used to sneak food to infirm Jews in Kaunas.

Faigie's father was killed in Dachau. "My mother and I—we were the only survivors of the family," said Faigie. She herself spent several years in a displaced persons camp before being allowed entry into Canada.

For dozens of years, Faigie refused to speak about her nightmare experiences. "I didn't speak to anybody. Maybe I didn't want people to feel bad. I don't know. Everybody knew I was a refugee," she said. "I didn't want them to live through what I lived through."

So now—I had the goods on two Nazi war criminals—Helmut Rauca and Haralds Puntulis—both of whom, ironically enough, lived within blocks of each other.

I used to wonder, do these bloodthirsty killers know each other? Did they pass each other on their walks in the neighborhood, and like proper European gentlemen, nod politely, unaware of the other's identity?

Arrest Rauca or Else...

The first thing Monday morning back in Canada, I called several Canadian government and police officials to demand they bring Helmut Rauca to justice on charges of aiding and abetting in the slaughter of more than 11,584 Lithuanian Jews.

I contacted the prime minister's office, the ministry of justice, the solicitor general, the ministry of external affairs, the immigration and passport department, and the RCMP.

"I know that the Nazi war criminal Helmut Rauca is living in Canada." Then I issued a threat: "If you don't arrest Rauca within seven days, I will tell the world how the Canadian government is protecting a mass murderer in its midst. If you continue to cover up for Rauca and protect him—when I expose the truth—Rauca will escape to Paraguay, and I will tell the world you let this killer escape on your watch!"

I didn't sense that any government officials cared, really. I was wrong.

That Monday evening, I received a phone call from Allan Waters, owner of the CHUM Network. Allan Waters was calling me? Why? I wasn't even aware that he knew who I was.

Mr. Waters said, "Jeff, what are you working on?"

"Well, Mr. Waters, I'm working on a story about Nazi war criminals who live in Canada."

"What have you got?" he asked.

"Well, I've got the goods and the documentation on two criminals who together murdered 16,000 people."

"You're confident in the information?" Mr. Waters asked.

"Yes, sir."

"Okay, Jeff. Full steam ahead!"

What I later discovered was that Mr. Waters had received a call from his high-level government contacts in Ottawa. Remember, the Trudeau government was in power and wanted nothing to do with a Nazi hunt.

The Americans were pissed at Canada—that's why they secretly gave the evidence to me. The US authorities should have been giving the evidence to the Canadian government, but no one in Canada had asked for it—except me.

That Thursday, three days after my ultimatum to the government—Helmut Rauca, a Canadian citizen, was arrested at his home in Willowdale.

That's when Faigie discovered Rauca was not only in Canada but was also living in Toronto. Near her home, in fact.

"I was horrified to discover that this man, the notorious Nazi responsible for the murder of many of my family members and friends, had been living only blocks away from my North York home. I felt compelled to tell my story," said a shaken Faigie.

Faigie said she was ready to testify against Rauca. "They needed witnesses and asked if I would go to Germany. I decided to go and give witness."

Rauca was in a German jail when he died on the 42nd anniversary of the largest mass killing in Lithuania.

Though Faigie never testified, Rauca's capture and death changed her life.

My TV Debut...

The first story I reported on at CITY-TV was "Nazi War Criminals in Canada"—highlighting the news of Rauca's extradition.

Early that evening, I went to Rauca's home and brought with me a camera crew to record my news report so it could appear on CITY-TV. My plan was to record what's called a "stand-up" outside Rauca's house.

Standing in front of the Rauca home, I began: "Earlier today, former SS Master Sergeant Helmut Rauca was extradited to West Germany to stand trial for war crimes, the first time for a Canadian. During his two-day extradition trial, sworn affidavits told of Rauca's role in forcing thousands of Jews onto trucks to be shot. We even heard how Rauca once beat and shot a man he suspected of hiding a fork."

Just then, I was loudly interrupted by a Rauca roommate who appeared on the porch of their home. It was an old man standing at the top of the stairs up to his house.

"Get off my property, now!" he shouted, though I was careful to be standing on the sidewalk. Needing him to shut his mouth so I could finish recording my stand-up and get back to the newsroom, I yelled in my deepest, loudest, and most intimidating voice, "Get back in the house old man—you're not in Germany anymore!"

That seemed to quieten him down, or so I thought. I must say, it felt good saying that.

By this time, I noticed that neighbors were standing in front of their homes watching the action unfold in real time. I continued my on-camera stand-up.

"After three decades of living openly as a free man in Canada,

Rauca will now likely face the rest of his life behind bars. I'm Jeff Ansell for..."

Before I had the chance to finish the signoff, my camera person yelled "Look out!" I quickly spun around and Rauca's buddy was literally holding a pitchfork to my neck, at which point I said something quite stupid.

"Put that pitchfork down or I'll kill you, old man."

Excuse me? What did I just say? Did I really just threaten to kill a man on-camera in front of a street full of witnesses?

If anything suspicious were to happen to this old bastard in the next while, I would be a prime suspect.

"Give me the tape," I demanded of my cameraperson. I snatched the video recording and later took it home to destroy. Thankfully, it was in the pre-Twitter days!

So, Helmut Rauca was taken care of.

One more Nazi to go.

Taking Down Puntulis...

My attention now turned back to telling the Puntulis story.

My thirty-minute investigative documentary on Puntulis was broadcast not only on *In Toronto* but also on the CHUM Radio Network, which extended from Vancouver to Halifax. However, the story of Haralds Puntulis deserved more attention than that. I wanted to tell the story to an even larger national audience—maybe even an international one as well. Keep in mind, no one had heard of the worldwide interweb yet.

I decided to write a lengthy, in-depth article about it for a newspaper or magazine. After twelve weeks of painstaking work writing an investigative article, I finally had a story that satisfied me. Article in hand, I went in search of a publisher.

First came the newspapers—the *Globe and Mail, Toronto Star, Toronto Sun*—but no one would touch the story for fear of potential lawsuits.

Next, I tried *Maclean's*, a national news magazine. "We'll take your article," they said.

I was ecstatic!

"In fact, we'll make it a cover story."

Wow! My heart leaped. That truly was beyond my expectations.

"There's just one thing. We can't publish your Nazi's name," they told me.

My heart fell. "What's the point?" I said. "Forget it." Puntulis, the killer, had to be named.

I proceeded to contact every credible publication I could think of—no success.

> *I went to the* Canadian Jewish News, *thinking for sure they would run the article. I didn't even want money for the piece. I would give it to them—or anyone—for free. I just wanted the story to be published. The editor of the CJN at the time, Maurice Lucow, refused to run the piece.*
>
> *Funnily enough, years later, I was invited to Vancouver to speak with the local chapter of the Canadian Jewish Congress. I told the story of how the CJN turned down the Puntulis story.*
>
> *That's when I was interrupted by a voice in the back row. It was Maurice Lucow.*
>
> *"My bosses wouldn't let me run your story," he said. "There was too much at risk from a liability perspective."*

I was baffled—I had the evidence, I had street cred—but it didn't matter. Media outlets wouldn't budge, and nobody wanted the story.

Finally, an idea dawned on me. The most widely read magazine in the country was *Today Magazine,* Canada's equivalent of the Sunday *New York Times Magazine.*

Today was distributed every Saturday in eighteen Canadian newspapers and had a national readership, interestingly enough, of six million. The magazine felt like a natural fit.

Why had I contacted them last? Because it never occurred to me to contact them earlier. Besides, *Today Magazine* was big.

Almost as a last resort, I contacted the magazine and spoke to the managing editor and well-respected writer Walter Stewart.

"Mr. Stewart, my name is Jeff Ansell. I'm an investigative reporter. I've been hunting Nazi war criminals in Canada for the last twelve months and have got the goods on two of them. Do you want the story, sir?"

"You know, this happens to be a real passion of mine too," Stewart said. "For the last several years, I've been gathering information on one particular Nazi, but I still haven't got enough."

"What's his name?" I asked.

"Haralds Puntulis," replied Stewart.

Bingo! My instincts were right. This was the right place. I sent Stewart my story. He said he was hoping to make my piece the issue's cover story, especially because we had access to Puntulis' Aizsargi pass, proving Haralds's Nazi creds.

After at least a dozen grueling re-writes with help from my brother-in-law Paul Appleby, the article was to appear in *Today Magazine*. We were riding high!

Then, I got hit by two torpedoes. First came the news that *Today Magazine* was closing down. Holy cow—what did that mean for my story? I immediately contacted Walter.

"We'll feature your Nazi article in the final issue," Walter told me. "But not as the cover story. Our final issue is slated to feature Mordecai Richler on the cover."

"A Richler cover story is predictable," I argued. "Why not put my Nazi article on the cover and go out with real impact and relevance?"

Walter was non-committal. Well, at least the article was going to appear somewhere!

The second torpedo struck when I received a phone call from Ben Kayfetz, a Jewish community leader who was aware of my work pursuing Puntulis.

"Jeff, did you read the obits this morning?" Ben asked. Not normally a practice of mine. I said no, but instantly knew why he was calling. Puntulis must be dead.

Sure enough, I checked the obituary section of the *Toronto Star*. "PUNTULIS, Haralds—Suddenly at home, on Sunday, July 4, 1982. Haralds, dear husband of Anna. Born in Latvia on May 14, 1909, immigrated to Canada in 1948 and engaged as a building contractor for 34 years. He will be especially missed by neighbors and children near his home."

My heart sunk. The motherfucker had the nerve to die on my watch.

I Don't Believe He's Dead...

Puntulis was as strong as a horse. He knew I was after him. Maybe he faked his death.

The "funeral" was that evening. I told Annie I believed Puntulis was alive and needed to go to his funeral to know for sure. Afraid I would make a scene at the funeral, Annie and Paul joined me.

I wanted to make a statement at the funeral, so I walked in wearing a torn T-shirt, ripped jeans, and my Chai necklace over my shirt. The necklace was a gift from my mother—the Chai is a symbol of the Jewish faith and means life.

It was clearly evident we did not belong, but I wanted everyone to see that despite Puntulis' effort to wipe us out, there were Jews at his funeral.

At one point, while Puntulis was being eulogized, I actually felt empathy for the widow Anna. Then, I quickly snapped out of it. After all, she was there with him through all of it.

At the end of the service, I still didn't believe Puntulis was dead. So, I opened his coffin.

Sure enough, Puntulis was in there. Dead as a doornail.

I remember being very angry in that moment. My heart began to beat rapidly, and my head felt like it was on fire.

The son of a bitch Puntulis had escaped justice. Unlike the people he slaughtered, he was allowed to live the high life—the bastard escaped scot-free.

But as I stood there looking over his body, a new sensation washed over me. Puntulis did not escape justice in the end. In his final send-off, I was there to represent the five-thousand-plus people he slaughtered, including the eleven-year-old boy. Puntulis may have been dead, but his crimes against humankind will never be forgotten.

Fittingly enough, after the funeral, Puntulis' body was shipped to the crematorium across the street from the funeral home. Unfortunately, when they put Puntulis inside the oven, he was already dead.

Forgive my selfishness, but at this point I wondered what Puntulis' death would mean for my article.

I brought *Today Magazine*'s Walter up to date on Puntulis dying and decided we could save the article if I slightly restructured it.

So, I re-wrote the article, starting it off with:

"It's the first Saturday in July and Harry is in his garden, admiring the shrubbery…"

The first Saturday in July was the last full day of Puntulis' life.

I amended the article's closing paragraph to reveal his death the next day. Walter liked the idea. The article was still a go.

August 28th, 1982, my article was the featured cover story in *Today Magazine*'s final issue. A collector's piece for sure![15]

Today Magazine cover

Circling Back...

Years later, I emailed Howard Blum, author of *Wanted! The Search for Nazis in America*. Howard is the one who helped get me started on my Nazi hunt, along with Mr. Wiesenthal.

I sent Howard the link[16] to me on YouTube talking about the genesis of the Nazi investigation, referencing his book, of course. (You may notice I buggered up the page number in the YouTube piece.)

Blum immediately wrote me back. He read my story in *Today* and said it was both important and well written. He added that it was a brave piece too.

Confronting Israel on Nazis...

As I had hoped, the article garnered international attention. In fact, the Israeli government invited me to meet with its top Justice Ministry official in Jerusalem, who was in charge of pursuing Nazi war criminals.

When we met, I challenged him. "Why do you expect us in the West to hunt Nazi war criminals while you in Israel are silent? Why isn't Israel doing something? Anything?"

"Israel is doing something," the official said. "We have our own ways of taking action. We just don't talk about it."

I took that to mean Israel was silently knocking off these murderers hidden across the globe.

"That's fine," I said, "only it's time for the world to see Israel publicly take action against living Nazi war criminals." Since the 1958 trial of key Hitler henchman Adolf Eichmann, Israel had kept a low profile on the Nazi war criminals' front.

"How can you expect us in North America, Europe, and Australia to pursue these war criminals when you're not seen to be taking any action?" I asked him again.

"Well, what do you suggest?"

"Why don't you publicly go after Josef Mengele?"

Mengele was the infamous chief doctor and "Angel of Death" at the Auschwitz-Birkenau concentration camp.[17]

"Offer a million-dollar reward for Mengele's capture," I suggested. The Justice Ministry official stopped to consider the reward idea. Then the conversation moved on.

Several months later, on the front page of the New York Times was the story of Israel offering a one million dollar reward for the capture of the Angel of Death. Apparently, I wasn't the only one who suggested the idea.

New York Times Mengele article headline

Israel Needs a Compelling Narrative…

Years later, I was disturbed by Israel's ongoing PR challenges, and it was clear Israel was in dire need of a narrative—or at least, a new narrative.

The Palestinian narrative didn't even require words. A picture of an Israeli soldier and a Palestinian youngster holding a rock told the whole story from the Palestinian perspective.

The Israeli narrative harkened back to the Balfour Declaration of 1917 and had the impact of one hand clapping.

Unsolicited, I created a public relations plan for the government of Israel and was once again invited to Jerusalem to share the details.

In the bowels of the Foreign Ministry, I sat at the largest boardroom table I have ever seen—it must have had close to forty seats, and they were all filled. I presented my plan to representatives of the prime minister's office, foreign affairs, the Justice Ministry, the Ministry of

Defense, the Israeli Defense Force, and a number of other government ministries, departments, and agencies.

To say I was intimidated is an understatement.

Israelis are an impatient lot from the get-go. They don't suffer fools, even those who cross the world to meet with them. I needed to make my presentation as relevant to them as it could be.

"I'm not some New York PR hotshot swooping in here to tell you how to improve your image," I said in my presentation's opening words. "Please cut me slack too if I mispronounce words or aren't familiar with an issue you bring up. What I have to say has nothing to do with your internal communications within Israel. I'm not qualified to do that," I said. "What I'm going to suggest reflects the international political picture and is designed for a global audience."

Every suggestion I made was met with support from one half of the room and derision from the other half. They argued with me, and they argued with each other.

"The highlight of my plan," I said, "is to have Israel's primary spokesperson to the world—be a Black woman." Remember, this was long before the Black Lives Matter movement and prior to Barack Obama's election.

Israel is home to more than 125,000 Black Jews, which represents the diversity of the Jewish people.

"Let's show this to a world that accuses Israel of practicing apartheid."

Of all the ideas I proposed, that was the only one everyone in the room supported. Mark Regev, who at the time was a top media adviser to the prime minister and later became the Israeli ambassador to the UK, told me he quite liked the idea and would pursue it.

Never happened.

An Idea For Germany...

When I joined one of the globe's top PR firms, Hill and Knowlton (now known as Hill + Knowlton Strategies), I had an idea for the government of Germany, one of our clients.

At the time, the German government faced an immigration crisis. In 1992, Germany admitted 306,600 asylum seekers.

I pitched my idea to our German team. "Given its past history and providing we can make a genuine case," I told them, "there's an opportunity to position Germany as the most humanitarian nation in Europe, if not the world."

Our office in Bonn quite liked the idea, though I don't know if they ever formally pitched it to the German government.

In the Movies...

More recently, I was asked to appear in the award-winning Canadian documentary *The Accountant of Auschwitz*. The producers asked me to be in the documentary because of my work on Puntulis and Rauca.

The Accountant of Auschwitz documented the story of ninety-three-year-old Oskar Gröning, whose role at the death camp was to collect the valuables of Jewish victims before they were marched into ovens. In 2014, Gröning was charged by German prosecutors as an accessory to murder in 300,000 cases. Despite his advanced age, the court ruled Gröning was still fit to stand trial.

The producers wanted my opinion on whether it's appropriate for such an old man to go to jail. I was reminded of what Simon Wiesenthal told me all those years ago when I asked about the rightness of jailing the elderly.

"When a criminal becomes old, does he stop being a criminal?" stated Mr. Wiesenthal.

My suggestion was that instead of being sent to prison, Gröning should be ordered to visit schools to share with youngsters the horrors of the Holocaust.

Gröning was sentenced to four years in prison—none of which he served. He died in the hospital at age ninety-six.

The Accountant of Auschwitz won four Canadian Screen Awards and, for a time, was available on Netflix, Amazon Prime, and CBC Gem.

A short time ago, Toronto commemorated Holocaust Education Week. To note the event, the Neuberger Holocaust Education Centre produced a video with me as the narrator. The whole video is worth watching.[18]

CHAPTER FIVE
Undercover Junkie

In 1980 while I was working at CHUM, a woman named Jane Ciriago called me. She lived in Parkdale, which at that time was a lower socio-economic community in Toronto.

"My husband Tony just died of a drug overdose. He was only 27," she said.

"He had this awful weakness for prescription drugs because they were easy to get and didn't cost as much as anything you could get on the street." Plus, she said, "They weren't cut with junk."

Tony kept promising to stop doing drugs. "You have a baby, and I won't drink, and I won't get high, which lasted about two weeks," Jane recounts.

What stands out in this story is not that Tony Ciriago was an addict—it was how easily he got the drugs that made him a junkie. At any one time, Tony was seeing two or three doctors on a weekly basis. He engaged in what's known as "double-doctoring."

"There are doctors in my neighborhood here who kept prescribing the drugs for Tony even though they knew he was an addict," she said. "The doctors had no medical reason for giving him the drugs. They just prescribed them to help him get high," she said.

"They have other patients like Tony," she told me. "I called the newspapers and TV and radio stations to tell them about these doctors, and no one will help me. Can you help me?"

"What would you like me to do?" I asked.

"Get these doctors off the street," she answered. "They're harming people, and my Tony is dead."

Thus, began our exploration into the last six months of Tony

Ciriago's life.

Had I received her call two years before, I too would have dismissed Jane as a crackpot and quickly gotten off the phone. This time was different.

We arranged to meet after work. Listening to Jane for a couple of hours convinced me that her story might be true. "Tony was visiting two doctors in particular," Jane recounted. "They knew he was a drug addict and they kept prescribing more and more pills, like Valium, Percodan, Tylenol 3, and other painkillers, just to get him high," she said. "There are a lot of other people being harmed by these two doctors—it wasn't just Tony."

To share the details of what Jane told me, I invited my fellow reporter Tim Laing to my place for dinner (Mandarin chicken, the only dish I knew how to prepare aside from French fries—and you already know how that turned out). From that very first night over dinner, Tim and I were clear about our end result—to prove these doctors contributed to Tony's death.

In preparing for this challenging assignment, we mapped out four steps, starting with the end in mind.

Step #4 Produce and broadcast a documentary called Pillers of Parkdale, highlighting negligent physicians responsible for patient deaths

Pillers of Parkdale was an ambiguous reference to the status and role of the physicians in the community.

Step #3 Gather evidence to substantiate our allegations, determine the laws and guidelines being violated, and see if the doctors unnecessarily prescribe drugs for us

Among others, we would need to interview medical experts knowledgeable about proper prescription protocols, regulators, lawyers, police, government officials, and above all—other people victimized by these physicians.

Step #2 Tim and I needed to become patients of the doctors

To do so, Tim and I would have to use our authentic government health cards. If we used fake health cards, we would have been committing fraud because the government was paying for the doctor visits, each of which was medically unnecessary.

Committing fraud to expose fraud would never wash in court.

Step #1 Prove Jane was telling the truth

Right now, all we had was her word to go on.

In order to learn the truth, there were a number of critically important questions and issues that needed to be addressed and answered. We would have to obtain verified documentation of the flow of drugs in her husband's name and identify the prescribing physicians.

Had these doctors actually prescribed the drugs? Which pharmacy had sold them? Did the pharmacists know they could be playing a role in killing customers? How would we get evidence from the pharmacy? How would we get in to see these doctors as patients? Was the government, which was paying for the drugs, aware it was being ripped off? Would health officials care?

We decided that our end result, if the story were true, would be a radio documentary to expose the actions of these doctors and their destructive impacts on people like Tony and Jane Ciriago.

Our challenges in the *Pillers* investigation were many, and Tim and I knew it would be a big undertaking. We both had full-time jobs on-air, and the station wasn't paying us extra to play Woodward and Bernstein. All of this work had to be on our own time, most of it during nights and weekends.

From beginning to end—research, interviews, undercover visits, writing and producing our documentary—the whole project took close to five months.

But first, we needed to prove Jane was telling the truth.

Accessing Private Medical Records...

The following week, I talked my way into the Parkdale drugstore where most of Tony's drugs had been prescribed.

"I'm the brother-in-law of Tony Ciriago," I told the pharmacist on duty. "He overdosed." The pharmacist held her breath for a moment and took a step back. "I'm sorry to hear that," she said with sincerity.

"We have a lot of different pills lying around the house, and my sister Jane and I need to know what the pills were in case her baby gets his hands on one. I need to see a record of Tony's prescriptions."

These were the days before today's heavy-duty privacy laws. Still, I was quite surprised when the pharmacist brought me around the counter to view the computer screen.

Standing there with a camera, I snapped away as each file came up on the computer detailing the drugs Tony had been prescribed, the dosage, the frequency, the volume, and by whom. Tony's prescription history revealed the names of the two Parkdale doctors who kept plying him with narcotics. We'll refer to them as Dr. A and Dr. B.

We now had proof that the two doctors in question had, over a period of months, prescribed enough drugs to kill Jane's husband several times over.

Becoming Patients...

The next step was to become patients of these two doctors. The original plan was for me to become a patient of Dr. A and for Tim to see Dr. B.

In order to become patients, we had to come up with ailments or symptoms that warranted a visit to their offices. Depression was our common theme.

Dr. A ran a storefront clinic in Parkdale. It was basically a one-man operation where it was first come, first serve. No appointments taken. The waiting room was nearly always jammed, with people either standing or sitting on worn, overstuffed furniture.

Dr. A's son handled the duty of shuffling patients from the waiting room into the doctor's office. The doctor also had an assistant who functioned as an errand boy and security guard—a bouncer, if you will.

Despite easy access to the waiting room, I discovered the doctor wouldn't see just anyone who walked in off the street. The problem was that Dr. A didn't take to me, as revealed in this secret recording of our conversation:

Jeff: Dr. A?
Dr. A: Yes

Jeff: Can I see you?
Dr. A: No, you don't see me. What do you want to see me about?

Jeff: I want to talk to you if I can. Do I need to make an appointment?
Dr. A: What would you like to see me about?

Jeff: I'm really feeling very uptight, doctor. I want to know if I can come in to see you.

Dr. A: No, I don't take new patients.
Jeff: You don't?
Dr. A: No.

Jeff: What do I have to do to see you?
Dr. A: I don't see new patients. With the money the government pays me per patient, I don't see new patients. I just have my old patients.

Jeff: How does somebody become an old patient?
Dr. A: How does somebody become a patient of mine? By being introduced by another patient whom I like. So, I don't see new patients.

On the other hand, Tim was able to establish a relationship with Dr. A, who went on to ply him with voluminous amounts of prescription drugs. I began visiting Dr. B, whose office was up the street from Dr. A.

On each visit, Tim and I were wired with a hidden microphone in the lining of our jackets while the other stood on the street outside, recording the doctor-patient conversation through the walls between us. Now it was time to catch the doctors in acts of grossly overprescribing narcotics.

Dr. B's very modest office needed a paint job and a good cleaning. He had no receptionist—just bikers in white lab coats manning the front desk. They would shout out "next" when it was time for another "patient/junkie" to see the doc.

My rapport, if you can call it that, with Dr. B was more successful. It was certainly weird, but he trusted me enough to cross several boundaries. When it was my turn with Dr. B, I had a story ready to go. Here are excerpts of my secretly recorded conversations with the doctor:

Jeff: I'm nervous as shit, doctor. If you'll excuse my French.

Dr. B: You're single, right?
Jeff: I'm single.

Dr. B: Nerves are bad?
Jeff: I'm very uptight.

Dr. B then took my blood pressure and said it was too high.

The closest I came to a full and proper examination, aside from the initial blood pressure test, was when Dr. B put a stethoscope to my chest, right up to where my microphone was hidden inside my jacket.

I was so scared at that moment that my heart was racing faster than a chicken with the colonel in hot pursuit. "Your heartbeat is high," Dr. B noted.

Dr. B: You come from a broken family or what?
Jeff: No.

Dr. B: How religious?
Jeff: Not very.

Dr. B: That's the problem. In this society, humans use drugs in order to calm ourselves. With all the frustration this society generates ... everybody wants pills to get high or get low or get sideways.

I hadn't asked for drugs at this point.

Dr. B: Our youth are starting to give up. The suicide rate is increased for everybody. The point is this—our society is hell-bent on destruction, partly by our insistence that we should get something without a cost.

Jeff: I know that feeling.
Dr. B: I know, for instance, that I had that feeling. I trained as a cardiologist—a specialist in the heart. I couldn't get the exams.

Jeff: Why?
Dr. B: I studied. I just didn't pass the exams. They wanted me to train for two more years to qualify for the exam ... you pin your hopes beyond your reach and society says you have hopes beyond your abilities.

The subject then turned to faith.

Dr. B: Jesus Christ frees you from your demands of your earthly body. The frustration you have can only be calmed by Jesus Christ. The demands of the body are to have food. The demand is to have sex. The demand is to have wealth.

Jeff: Uh-huh.

Dr. B: Pills are not the solution. Pills are just a crutch—a very poor crutch at best. I give you a few, okay?

Dr. B then gave me a choice of five- or ten-milligram strength. Naturally, I went for the ten. He prescribed forty pills.

Jeff: Can I get a little more, or can I come back and see you soon?
Dr. B: Yes, two weeks or so—ten days.

Jeff: Can I come back within a week?
Dr. B: Sure, ten days.

Jeff: Can I come back next week?
Dr. B: Yes.

After my so-called appointments with Dr. B, he would pick up a phone with a direct line to the pharmacy downstairs—no dialing required. It was the same pharmacy that allowed me access to Tony's prescription history.

Dr. B would simply say, "Ansell, Jeff—ten milligrams of Diazepam (Valium) for a fortnight."

Because I used my own name, as did Tim, we just hoped neither doctor was a CHUM listener.

Many times, I was so scared to visit Dr. B that I would smoke a joint beforehand. Here I was getting high, smoking a joint before going undercover to expose a drug-pushing doctor. But hey—he was the doctor, not me.

On my third visit to Dr. B, my "girlfriend" came up as a topic.

Dr. B: So, what about the girlfriend? Have you made up with her?
Jeff: Not yet.

Dr. B: How long you used to live with her?
Jeff: Year and a half.

Dr. B: She was good in bed, eh?

Jeff: (chuckles)

Dr. B: Man, did she have an orgasm! Wowee! Wow! Wow! Man, she sucks you right here—whoopie doopie doo!

Jeff: (laughs)

Dr. B: A nymphomaniac (whistles). Move like a silk in bed man, move like a silk. Rah! Rah! Rah! (shouting). It's tough to be without them and it's tough to be with them.

On my fifth visit, Dr. B raised concern about what appeared to be my excessive consumption of prescription drugs.

Dr. B: Are you taking too many pills?

Jeff: Yoo.

Moments later, he gave me more Valium.

The following week he told me for the first time that I was taking too much Valium. Then, he said it was habit-forming and he wouldn't prescribe it much in the future.

I listened, and then received my script for forty more Valium. A week after that I was in the doctor's office less than a minute when he picked up the phone and ordered me forty more Valium, for an overall total stash of 280 Valium pills.

During the course of our investigation, we discovered that within a four-week period, Dr. A had prescribed Tony Ciriago thirty units of the painkiller Indicid, a quantity of Percodan, forty units of Valium, and fifty units of Tylenol 3 (which packs a whammy).

The scripts were written in Jane's name.

Once, at a crucial moment in our gathering of evidence, Tim was in Dr. A's office and I was outside recording the conversation. Not getting a strong enough signal from Tim's microphone, I found that I could get better reception of the conversation in the lobby of the apartment building next door.

Tim's meeting with the doctor seemed to go on and on, and mid-way through, I had to go to the bathroom in the worst way! Tim and Dr. A were coming to the part where the doctor was about to give Tim the drugs. I needed to record that encounter! If I left now to find a restroom, months and months of work would have gone down the drain. So, I took care of my personal business right there in the lobby, hoping no one would catch me in the act.

Over the course of our visits, some sixteen in all, we never once asked for drugs, but the doctors prescribed voluminous amounts of pills for Tim and me.

Having gathered enough evidence, we were then ready for the next step—meet and interview regulators at the College of Physicians and Surgeons of Ontario, the Ontario College of Pharmacists, legal authorities, and government officials.

Following that, we produced and broadcasted our documentary *Pillers of Parkdale,* highlighting negligent physicians responsible for patient deaths.

The Fallout…

The day after the sixty-minute program aired on CHUM, federal drug agents swooped into the newsroom to seize all the drugs. RCMP actually counted each and every pill to ensure numbers matched and that no one had been dipping into the stash. All present and accounted for!

Disciplinary charges were laid, and I testified in court against Dr. B. Interestingly enough, the prosecutor in the case against Dr. B was John Tory, my radio colleague from CFTR and future mayor of Toronto.

During a break in the proceedings, I found myself in the restroom with the doctor's high-powered and expensive lawyer. The lawyer was known for being a tough cookie, and I didn't relish being cross-examined by him. He was likely to argue that his client was a victim of entrapment on my part.

As we stood beside each other washing our hands, I thought to myself that I'm probably not allowed to talk to him outside the courtroom.

However, several days before, I had read that he was helping fund important research to find water in the deserts of the Middle East. I thought it was fascinating. So, I said to him, "That project you're involved with in the Middle East sounds really exciting. How's it going?"

I could see that he was very uncomfortable talking to me. He paused for a moment and then said, "It's going very well. Thank you very much for asking." And he walked out.

Later in the day, it came time for me to testify, but rather than it being the ordeal I'd expected, I found the lawyer's cross-examination to be remarkably gentle and I got through it unscathed. Dr. B was found guilty of failing to maintain the standard of practice of the profession, making improper use of the authority to prescribe, dispense, or sell a drug, and professional misconduct.

Though Dr. B received a three-month suspension resulting from my visits with him, years later he was tossed out of medicine altogether after being found guilty of groping a female patient.

Why did Dr. B and Dr. A turn on the drug taps for the junkies in the neighborhood? Maybe they actually believed they were doing well by their patients—helping them cope with the challenges of everyday life. I can only speculate.

Tim and I had the good fortune of winning the Radio & TV News Directors Association award for the "Most Significant Contribution to the Improvement of News Gathering" in the country.

Tim Laing & Jeff

On a larger scale, *Pillers of Parkdale* was nominated for the Michener Award, presented by the governor general of Canada, to whom the prime minister reports. The Michener Award is one of the highest distinctions in Canadian journalism. The award honors news organizations and journalists who have made "a significant impact on public policy or on the lives of Canadians."

Governor General Edward Schreyer & Jeff

In the photo, you'll notice the governor general has one hand behind his back. It's because he's holding a glass of scotch.

When we accepted the award from Canada's governor general, I couldn't help but flash back to the apartment lobby situation.

The story behind the story.

CHAPTER SIX

Broken Homes

Investigative reporting and the *Pillers of Parkdale* reinforced in me the power I had to make a difference in people's lives.

After receiving a tip about deplorable conditions at a downtown Toronto nursing home, I began an investigation that lasted several months. My findings resulted in a thirty-minute TV documentary entitled *Nursing Homes: The Promise of Age.*

Thankfully, in the course of my investigation, I found that most homes were well maintained. However, some nursing homes weren't—and one run-down home is one too many. The bad-apple nursing home I homed in on was called St. Raphael's. Close to 120 seniors, many infirm, lived there.

From the outside, St. Raphael's exterior was exquisite. Originally built in 1901 as the old Mount Sinai Hospital, it was a stately, white-stone building on Yorkville Avenue, a very elegant part of Toronto. [19]

The exterior of the nursing home was so beautiful that people would stop just to look at it. Inside, the home was a rat's nest. The structure was unsafe and badly in need of repair.

In addition to having high rates of bedsores, the residents had emergency call buttons that didn't work. What were the oldsters to do if they needed help in an urgent situation? Simply yell for help? The call buttons were critical to attentive care.

The folks who called St. Raphael's home were simply women and men unable to fight back or care for themselves. They were depen-dent on private nursing homes and profit-oriented owners looking to save a dime wherever possible, caring little, if at all, for the well-being of their residents. They—the residents—were the ones who paid the price.

By hook or by crook, I needed to get in there. I had a few different options for gaining access.

The first and quickest option was to force my way into the home, camera rolling—which I tried. But three of the home's personal aide workers were tugging on the door from the inside, fiercely trying to keep me out. I managed to pull the door open and all three aides came flying out. It made for great television—but didn't help the residents, which was the whole intent.

So, I tried a second approach.

Sweet-Talking My Way In...

I contacted the administrator of the nursing home. "I'm working on a documentary about our senior years—what we can look forward to as we grow older, and so on. I'd love to do an interview with you to talk about physiotherapy for seniors, diet, recreation at the home, and so on."

She agreed to the interview.

True to my word, I began the interview by lobbing softball questions.

"What's life like at St. Raphael's?" I asked innocently.

"Uh-huh, and what types of activities do the residents engage in? Is there a regular exercise program?"

By now, the administrator's guard was down. Then, I hit her with:

"Why do you neglect your residents? Why do so many residents have bedsores? Why are your emergency call buttons broken? Is your home unsafe?"

The administrator was bamboozled and tied up in knots. I got what I needed from her.

But I still needed proof—eyewitness accounts, for instance.

Planting a Spy...

So, I tried yet another approach to gain entry into St. Raphael's—to place a spy inside the home. In recruiting the spy, however, I was less than forthcoming about my motives.

My friend Gary had a lot of free time, so I mentioned there might be an opportunity for him to volunteer at St. Raphael's nursing home downtown.

I never told Gary a word about the conditions inside. I left that for him to tell me—and he did.

Gary's work as a volunteer at St. Raphael's confirmed the home's decrepit environment and neglectful atmosphere. "Jeff, this place is bad," he said. "The residents are ignored. They're forced to lie in their own waste for hours. The place is an absolute hell-hole."

A week or so later, Gary phoned me with yet another upsetting update.

"Jeff, you're not going to believe what just happened here," Gary said. "The residents were finishing lunch and leaving the dining room when the ceiling collapsed! Thankfully, no one was in there when the roof caved in, but if it had happened a few minutes earlier, people would have been killed."

That evening, I took the St. Raphael story to Ontario's minister of health, responsible for the entire health care system, including nursing homes. I shared with him my evidence. I told him about the ceiling collapse, which he personally did not know about.

Authorities acted so swiftly in closing the home that it happened before I could even put the documentary on television.

The day St. Raphael's Nursing Home closed, I stood on a balcony across the street and recorded the whole event. I filmed as yellow buses swooped in to move these folks to new and better homes across the city.

They were checking out of this hell-hole, hopefully to nursing homes where they would receive the care they deserved and be treated like human beings.

As the residents walked or were wheeled out onto the street, they were happy. It was a heartwarming, inspiring moment—a memory I will have forever. And I was there to capture it for others to see.

As a result of that program, laws changed, including one that compelled all nursing homes to have emergency call buttons that actually work.

Care for a Kid Named Kevin...

The *In Toronto* program on CHUM provided me with a venue for in-depth interviews and human-interest stories.

Disturbed by low adoption statistics, I prepared a thirty-minute program that focused on kids in foster care, like eight-year-old Kevin, a foster child shunted from home to home who confirmed my purpose in being a reporter.

Kevin's birth mother used to beat him viciously. Thus, at a very early age, he was removed from her care and sent to live with a number of foster parents.

Child Services introduced me to Kevin. By the time I met him, Kevin had lived in a handful of homes that didn't take. In creating my documentary on adoption and foster care, I spent many hours with Kevin, walking, talking, and listening to what life looked like through his eyes. I also interviewed childcare experts, psychologists, and others with insights into the system.

But the real story was this young boy. Alone in the world, knocked around by life—Kevin needed a loving home.

Toward the end of my documentary on Kevin, I asked him, "What do you want more than anything else?"

"A family," he said.

"And what are you going to do when you're older?" I wondered.

"I'm going to adopt!"

By the time I put Kevin's story on the radio, I felt pretty close to the youngster. Though I was in my early twenties, I myself wanted to adopt a child. Because I was so young and not ready (or eligible) to do so, I opted to be a Big Brother instead.[20]

A day or two after Kevin's program was broadcast, I went back to see him in his foster home and brought with me a copy of his story on audiotape. Since he didn't have a tape machine to play it on, I bought him a cassette recorder as well.

"Kevin, I've got something for you."

"A bike?!" he asked excitedly.

"No. A tape of your story and a tape machine to listen to it on."

(I wish I brought him a bike instead.)

Sitting together on the edge of his bed, I played him his story. Here was a boy who'd been bashed around by life, who at a tender age had lived most of his years in "the system."

The last memory I have of Kevin was of him standing beside my car as I was about to drive away. We said our goodbyes.

Though I felt sad driving away, Kevin had this big smile on his face. Thoughts of him pierced me as I drove home, and I began to reflect.

Kevin knew that when he got older, he was going to bring kids like himself into his home. Kevin's story helped me further appreciate the potential impact reporters have in ways to help people and touch their lives in a genuine, meaningful way. I hope I did that for Kevin.

I know he did it for me.

Though I never found out what eventually happened to Kevin, my heart hopes he found a kind, loving home. If Kevin or any other youngster found a happy home because of that story, it would be the highlight of my career.

More than that—it would be one of the highlights of my life.

CHAPTER SEVEN
Walking Away from My Dream

There was a time in my life as a reporter when I would cry almost every day. I'd meet people who were going through the horrors of life, having the most tragic experiences, and I'd have to tell their stories on TV. Then, on the way home from work, alone in my car, I would simply start to weep.

I was assigned to cover a story about a five-year-old boy, Paul, who was ill with leukemia. The family had tried various treatments here in Canada, and nothing worked.

Paul's dad, a postal worker, was raising money for his son to receive specialized medical treatment in the United States. So, his co-workers held a barbecue outside of the post office depot where he worked, and they raised some cash.

Everyone came: the guys who were off-shift, their families, their friends. A cameraperson and I drove to the event where we took general shots of the barbecue and me mixing it up with people.

Paul's mom and dad were decent people, salt of the earth. What they were going through was no doubt so incredibly painful. I remember going up to them and asking, "Do you mind if I talk to your boy alone?"

Then, the two of us went in search of a quiet spot. I went for a walk with Paul—truly a lovely boy. Finding a space to ourselves, we sat down on some steps.

The camera was about thirty feet away, and I was wired with a mic. We talked for about twenty minutes, though I only used thirty seconds of our conversation on air. I wanted to preserve the rest of our conversation just for Paul's family to see and cherish privately.

I brought them a video copy of my conversation with Paul so they would have another memory of their boy.

After reporting the story, I was overwhelmed with sadness. I edited the story back in the studio and put it on TV. And on the way home, I broke down.

Paul died three weeks later. I went to visit the family, and we sat at the kitchen table and drank Pepsi and talked about the boy.

"Your son was very special," I said.

The boy "was courageous to the end," Paul's dad said.

Stories like the one about Paul ripped up my insides. I still think of Paul and his family today.

In spite of my avenging reporter persona, I was never totally comfortable with the invasive nature of the work. There were many times when I felt my presence at a news event was an intrusion on the people affected.

I remember attending a murder scene when the victim's father discovered reporters outside his daughter's apartment. I knew what had happened to his daughter. He didn't. It was painful to witness.

"What happened?" he cried out to me. "Did something happen to my daughter?" he demanded to know.

"The authorities might have information for you," I suggested, dipping my head down. I couldn't look him in the eye.

For me, this was a devastating moment to witness. For my fellow reporters on the scene, it was just another day at the office.

Musician Don Henley was bang on with "Dirty Laundry," his hit song about the news business—specifically, about news anchors who worry more about their looks than they do about the news or its repercussions.

"See the bubble-headed bleached-blonde, comes on at five," Henley sings. "She can tell you 'bout the plane crash with a gleam in her eye."[21]

Here I was, knocking on people's doors and shoving a microphone in their face asking, "How does it feel?" just as they're going through the worst moments in their lives.

That is what reporters are supposed to do. As the saying goes in the news business, "if it bleeds, it leads."

But I felt like a vulture. Going after bad guys was one thing. But pouncing on innocent people when they were vulnerable, weak, and confronting life's most horrible experiences was another.

I just wasn't comfortable with that anymore.

The Straw That Broke...

Then one day, a single incident pushed me out the newsroom door.

I was anchoring the 6 p.m. news on a very slow news day. We used to call them "the dog days of August" because there was always very little news happening.

All we had for our top story was a stabbing victim in critical condition in hospital. It wasn't a strong lead, and I hated to open with stories about crime because it made for tabloid-like newscasts.

The tension grew as we moved toward airtime on this hot, muggy afternoon. Then, at 5:30 p.m., the assignment editor got on the loudspeaker.

"Good news," he announced to our big, gymnasium-style newsroom. "We have a lead story. The stabbing victim died." People in the newsroom erupted into a cheer!

That was all I needed. I got up, walked across the newsroom floor into Moses' office, and quit.

On the way home, it hit me—what did I just do?

What am I going to tell Annie? That I quit my TV job because everyone clapped for a news headline? What kind of reason is that to quit? She's going to kill me!

As it turned out, Annie couldn't have been more supportive.

It was time for me to move on to new adventures in my life with new stories yet to come.

Stories where I would hopefully still have the opportunity to impact others in a good way.[22]

CHAPTER EIGHT

What's a Media Trainer?

Needing to earn a living, I now wanted to teach people how to deal with the Jeff Ansells of this world. As a media trainer and public affairs adviser, I could take all that I'd learned as a reporter and apply it where it might make an actual difference.

Instead of just reporting on what companies were doing, maybe I could now influence them—by helping shape their policies from the inside.

Media training is a process to equip anyone who interacts with media with skills and techniques to respond to tough questions—on the spot—without blowing their big toe off.

The process involves the delivery of honest responses, meaningful messages, and ways to rectify bad situations. This applies not only with media but also with critical stakeholders like investors, government, customers, and employees.

Many people wonder why there is a need for media trainers when all newsmakers and interviewees need to do is tell the truth. When dealing with the media, however, the truth is not good enough. The back and forth between reporters and the people they interview can often be a stilted, scheming, conniving dynamic that comes naturally to no one, me included.

When speaking to news reporters (especially ones like me), it is too easy for people in the news to step on their tongues. It happens every day.

Consider, for instance, this exchange between a reporter and an executive representing a charity:

Question: "Are you still stealing money from the charity?"

Answer: "I hold myself to high standards of integrity. I have never stolen money from my charity."

Now, imagine you're a reporter—which of the interviewee's two sentences would you quote?

The first sentence, "I hold myself to high standards of integrity," is fine—if it's true. But you don't need a Columbia journalism degree to know which sentence the reporter will gravitate to.

The second sentence, "I have never stolen money from my charity," if used as the only quote in the story, re-iterates the ugly allegation, even though the executive may very well be innocent.

In today's cancel culture, it is too simple for a reputation to be ruined by a misguided and defensive turn of phrase or an ill-thought-out statement delivered on the spot.

Social media has made this world an awful lot smaller, too. As my old boss Bob Holiday used to say, "No sooner done than said." Again—that was long before the internet. Gone are the days when newsmakers could easily manipulate and mislead the media.

I wanted to give media training a go. I approached Hill and Knowlton, one of the world's top public relations companies. With very few discussions, they invited me to become director of their national communications training division, which up until then hadn't existed. I jumped at the opportunity.

Being at Hill and Knowlton was like stepping into the major leagues, and with that feeling came trepidation. Interviewing and reporting had been great, but what I discovered was that anybody could ask questions. An equal-or-greater skill lay in answering them honestly with simple to understand messages that allowed for control of context.

In media coaching, I would first interview executives, asking them my toughest questions, then feed back to them that which they had said.

No longer simply the interrogator, however, I was also the one who was going to help them respond. Moving from reporter to coach, the stakes became much higher. I was now suggesting what people ought to say and do, and with that came responsibility.

It humbled me that people actually thought I knew what I was talking about. That made me think twice about what I said.

After all, what if they ended up taking my advice?

Trying to Do What's Right...

One particular incident helped me realize the influence I could potentially have on corporations.

An industrial client had just been purchased by a larger firm and needed to institute layoffs. On this assignment, my role was to coach the executives on how to talk to employees and the media about the acquisition and the upcoming layoffs.

It was two weeks before Christmas. Most of the employees to be let go were single mothers, and the CEO's plan was to provide the workers with the minimal number of benefits required by legislation.

Listening to him that morning, I suddenly had visions of what it must have been like for my father when the owners of his clothing factory let him go after fifty years. I recall how he used to just sit at the kitchen table on days he should have been working. He was like a fish out of water. Layoff issues were difficult for me.

I thought about the client in front of me. How can your company do this? You're not suffering for money. My mind started to race. How will I convince the executive team to do what's right by their employees, especially at this time of year? How can I get them to keep employees working well past Christmas, plus extend their benefits?

The people who were to be let go had kids who need clothes, food, braces, and maybe a Christmas present thrown in.

I knew if I tried to appeal to the CEO on that level, it wouldn't work—it would have minimal impact. I would be seen as naïve. So, I had to use my skills as a reporter to make him see the light.

Here's a sampling of the questions I asked and the answers the CEO gave.

Jeff: Wouldn't you consider it heartless to lay off your employees just before Christmas?

CEO: We're not heartless. It's just business in today's world.

Jeff: Why are you skimping on benefits?

CEO: We're not.

Jeff: You're not what?

CEO: We're not skimping on benefits. We're meeting the minimum requirements.

Jeff: So, you don't think you're acting like Scrooge?

CEO: No, I don't think I'm acting like Scrooge.

Need I tell you the quotes that would make into to media?

"We're not heartless," insists defensive CEO.

"We're not skimping on benefits," CEO claims.

"I'm not acting like Scrooge," said the angry CEO.

I asked him, "How would you feel seeing those quotes in the media?"

"Not good," he tersely answered.

The CEO sat there silently for a couple of moments in front of a boardroom full of people. Then, he reached for a phone and called his top HR person. "We're moving the layoffs past Christmas," he said. "And I want their benefits extended another six months."

I was astonished and very happy the employees would at least have jobs past the holidays. I'm grateful to have had the opportunity to hopefully have a bit of a positive impact on people I would never meet.

When Eaton's, a huge Canadian department store chain, began gutting locations, I met a top-ranking member of the Eaton family as he and his large entourage of fancy suits were walking out of one of their stores as I was walking in.

I recognized him, introduced myself, and explained what I do for a living. "I work with executives and leaders to convey trust and to help deliver difficult messages at tough times," I said.

That prompted Eaton to ask, "So, how did I do?"

He caught me by surprise. I wasn't quite sure what to say. But I figured, you know what? This is my kick at the can. When am I going to get a member of the Eaton family in front of me again? I don't care if he likes what I'm going to say—he's not a client anyway.

"Well, I'll tell you the truth," I said. "You talked so much about Eaton's money problems, but never once did I hear you say 'thank you' to those people who've given you the best years of their working lives. People have shopped in your family's stores for generations. In the last week, did you once publicly say 'thank you' to your customers?"

He looked at me, smiled, and walked away. Two days later, the company came out with ads that said, "Thank you."

"I don't know if those ads were a result of our encounter or whether they were already in the works—but they represented the right thing to do.

Media Trainees...

Over the course of my six years at Hill and Knowlton, and later at my own firm, Jeff Ansell & Associates, I provided media, crisis, and presentation training to many thousands of people around the world.

My clients over the years include famous athletes, political leaders, big tech execs, two Supreme Court justices, two Walmart CEOs, and a host of *The View*.

I even media trained Carl Bernstein.

Voter.com was a website dedicated to exploring politics at every level. The Washington DC-based company was created by the founders of *George* magazine, which was established by John F. Kennedy Jr. A representative of Voter.com heard of my work and called me.

"Jeff, we want you to work with the owner of the company, two key advisors, and our new partner, Carl Bernstein."

"Carl Bernstein from Watergate?" I asked.

"Yeah, that Carl Bernstein," he replied. "Carl's now the executive editor of Voter.com, and he'll be at our next meeting in Washington."

He continued, "We want you to train Carl in dealing with the media, as well as Randy Tate (former president of the Christian Coalition) and Craig Smith (former political director of the Clinton White House). We're also bringing a dozen observers."

I was terrified. What could I teach Carl Bernstein about the news media? He was my inspiration for wanting to be an investigative reporter in the first place. Everybody knows about Watergate and the movie *All the President's Men*. Dustin Hoffman played Carl in the movie, and Robert Redford played Woodward.

This is going to be a tough assignment, I thought. If Carl, Randy, and Craig were alone with me in the room, no problem. I could deal with it—scared as I was. But I would have a studio audience behind me, and the three of them were, no doubt, conscious of the audience as well and not wanting to look foolish in front of them. Yet, it was my job to make them look foolish and say dopey things.

When the training program kicked off, I started to relax a bit when one of the trio of trainees wrote down something that I had said. It was a positive sign.

As for Carl, I felt I needed to be aggressive, in part, to ensure I had his full attention. But I didn't want to embarrass Carl—so I decided to give him a heads up by starting interviews with Randy and Craig.

I'd throw them to the wolves first. I tossed Randy a provocative question, the kind he might get from a hostile reporter, in an attempt to interrogate and fluster him. Same with Craig. It worked well.

Then, it was Carl's turn to answer my questions. He could be really good at this, I thought. In which case, I didn't know what value I could offer him.

My first question to Carl was, "So, tell me how your career went downhill after Watergate?"

Carl immediately pushed back at me. "My career has not gone downhill," he barked.

At that moment, I knew everything was going to be okay. It was exactly the kind of answer the news media loves to get because it's so quotable and ripe with conflict, though none actually exists.

Unfortunately, the person being interviewed doesn't get a second chance to give a better first impression. But that was why I was there, to train them in mastering communication with the media. From then on, everyone became willing participants.

Before going to the meeting in Washington, I picked up copies of *All the President's Men* for Carl to autograph. When the training was done, Carl came over.

"The session was great. I had no idea how to answer some of those questions you asked."

Carl, now a CNN political analyst, autographed the books and we went out for drinks.

Carl Bernstein & Jeff

Training a Tough Guy...

One athlete I media trained was Todd Bertuzzi of the Vancouver Canucks. A dozen other players joined us as well.

In a game with the Colorado Avalanche, Bertuzzi grabbed opponent Steve Moore, punched him in the back of the head, and then slammed Moore's head on the ice. Moore was unconscious and lay still on the ice for ten minutes. Two days later, Bertuzzi wept publicly and apologized for what had happened.

Though he eventually recovered, Moore's hockey career was over.

Bertuzzi paid quite the price too. He received a seventeen-month suspension, the loss of hundreds of thousands of dollars in endorse-ment deals, and he faced a criminal-assault charge and a civil lawsuit.

When I trained Bertuzzi, he scared the crap out of me. When I asked him questions like, "Were you trying to kill Moore?" he angrily glared at me. I honestly thought he might jump across the table and knock me unconscious.

In the end, Bertuzzi was a complete gentleman and even brought out a Sharpie, offering to sign a Bertuzzi jersey I'd brought with me as a souvenir for my son.

By the way, we did the training in the team's dressing room. It was the only time I ever conducted a training session within three feet of a urinal.

Like Magic...

When the NBA was expanding to Canada, the league had to decide which of three bids to accept. I worked on the bid spearheaded by Michael Cohl, organizer of concert tours for the Rolling Stones. Joining Cohl on the bid was famed NBA legend, Magic Johnson.

When Magic and I first shook hands, my hand just disappeared into his. It was like shaking hands with Paul Bunyan.

I asked Magic what I should call him. "Call me Earvin," he gra-ciously said.

The plan was to rehearse for the next day's news conference, but Earvin had other plans. "I'm good without doing the rehearsal," he insisted. "I deal with media all the time. I don't need to practice. I'm good at it."

Wouldn't you know it? Magic buggered up. Asked whether he would work with the winning bidder if his group lost, Magic said yes—without realizing he was undermining confidence in the Cohl bid.

The media jumped on his comment, suggesting it showed a lack of confidence in his own bid. It took us days to undo and showed us all how careful we had to be when it comes to answering unexpected questions. All Magic needed to say was, "Our bid will give Toronto a championship team!"

Here are two other tidbits I recall from Magic's Toronto news conference.

First, women came up to me with tiny slips of paper with their phone numbers for me to pass on to Magic. This, even though Magic had contracted AIDS.

Plus, when Magic took the stage, he wore a beautifully tailored suit. I kept thinking that if I tried on Magic's pants, the waist would come up my neck, if not higher.

Unfortunately for Cohl and Magic, their bid was defeated by the group that partnered with another ex-NBA great, Isaiah Thomas. Isaiah became the founding general manager of the Toronto Raptors basketball team.

I later media trained Isaiah.

What stands out about Isaiah from the brief time I spent with him was his under-the-radar style. I sensed that he wants people to underestimate him, which can serve him well, especially during a negotiation.

Mayor Rob Ford...

If anyone ever needed media training, it should have been Rob Ford, the Toronto mayor caught smoking crack on video. During a scrum, he actually referred to a sexual act he engaged in with his wife.

Mayor Ford was a train wreck, so when I got the call from City Hall to meet with him, I was quite intrigued. When I got there for our appointment, the mayor was nowhere to be found, so I met with Amir Remtulla, his chief of staff. Amir and I knew each other from his previous life at Molson.

"The mayor wants you to do his media training," Amir said. "But he doesn't want the city to pay for it."

"That's fine with me," I said. "I don't want the city to pay for it either."

Anytime a consultant does work for the government, the amount of money paid becomes public information. I'm a very private person, believe it or not. Or at least, I was until I sat down to write this book.

Then, Amir told me the mayor didn't want to pay either. So why was I there? Mayor Ford came from a wealthy family—so it wasn't a matter of not being able to afford me.

So, I called their bluff.

"I'll do it for free," I said.

Rob Ford never took me up on my freebie offer.

No One Ever Gets That Good...

Everyone needs to be put through the media training paces—including me. As good as I may be at teaching others how to deal with media, I myself have had the opportunity to screw up.

As part of a story he was preparing on the phenomena of "media training," *Toronto Star* reporter Bob Brehl came to me to be media trained.

"I want you to teach me what you teach your clients," said Brehl. "Help me learn how best to answer aggressive and trick questions."

So, I trained Bob, providing him, I hope, with insight into how easy it is for articulate people to say something upid-stay. For three hours, I rode shotgun over every word that left my lips, knowing anything I said could come back to haunt me in tomorrow's paper—and make me either look good or not so good.

Just as the session was over and I was at the finish line—in fact, at the front door saying goodbye—I said something really dumb to Bob and hoped I wouldn't see it in the article. I did.

There it was in the next day's *Toronto Star*. The quote was, "'I don't teach people how to lie,' claims Ansell."

So, none of us ever get *that good* at dealing with the media. Once we start thinking we're that good with the media, the more likely we are to blow our brains out.

By the way, Bob Brehl is now a media trainer.

CHAPTER NINE
Book Writing, Ventures, and Misadventures

In this era, more than others, knowing how to deal with the media is essential if you're in the public eye. That's why I dedicated years to writing a book about media and crisis communications that PR practitioners across the globe are hopefully benefiting from.

When the Headline Is You: An Insider's Guide to Handling the Media will be of great interest to those looking to master media and crisis communications skills.[23]

Though I came up with four steps to help me reach my goal—it didn't quite go as planned. Here's how I saw the creation of my book unfolding:

Step #1 Start writing

Step #2 Edit and revise until the manuscript is as good as I can make it

Step #3 Make a deal with a big publisher who can get me into Barnes & Noble and popular bookselling sites

Step #4 See myself in Barnes and Noble on 5th Avenue in New York holding a copy of my book

Thinking it might make my book offering more enticing, I sought out blurbs for the inside and back cover before approaching publishers. Blurbs are one or two sentences that speak to the wisdom and teaching offered in the book.

So, I got blurbs from, amongst others, the White House (I trained George W. Bush's communications director and several spokespeople), Harvard Business School, and public relations guru Richard Edelman, CEO of Edelman PR, the world's largest communications firm.

Knowing he might not be willing to provide a blurb, I made my ask of Edelman bigger, thinking I could work my way down. I asked if he would write the foreword to the book. If Edelman wrote the foreword, I would put his name on the book cover in the hope people would think he wrote it—thereby boosting sales.

I sent the manuscript to Edelman, and he wrote back saying he was too busy to craft a foreword but would happily provide a blurb. Here's what he graciously wrote for my back cover:

> *Business Media continue to be the most credible sources of information on companies. Jeff Ansell's book* When the Headline Is You *offers invaluable advice on managing relationships with these outlets.*

I should add that there were naturally obstacles along the way. Most publishers, big and small, turned me down. Amazingly, one didn't.

I sent the manuscript to John Wiley & Sons, one of the world's biggest publishing houses, and the next thing I knew—they sent me a contract and an advance. It was unbelievable! I was so proud of the advance that I copied the check, hung it on a wall above my desk, and told everybody that I'd scored a book deal with Wiley.

I gave myself a canary. A "canary" is a Yinglish word meaning I jinxed myself. It's when someone says, "I love your hair," and the next morning, your hair is all over the pillow.

The rug was pulled out from under me. My publisher called me (after I cashed the check) and threw me for a loop.

"We just read your book," they said.

"Excuse me?" I replied. "You just now read my book?"

"Yes, and we don't like it."

You know that feeling when your heart sinks? That's what happened.

"You wrote the book from an anecdotal perspective," the publisher's rep told me. "We want it to be more prescriptive."

"What does that mean?" I nervously asked.

"It means that instead of telling a story and then offering the learning from the story, start off with the learning and then tell the story.

"You have three choices," they went on to tell me. "The first is to send us our money back."

When I heard that, I stopped breathing.

"The second choice is to start over and rewrite the book." Not likely to happen on my part.

"The third choice is to work with an editor," they concluded. I'll take work with an editor for two hundred please, Alex.

Wiley then set me up with an editor named Jeffrey Leeson. Jeffrey provided guidance on how to restructure the book, but with new deadlines looming, I wasn't making enough progress. So, I asked Jeffrey to write the book with me, instead of merely advising me.

"I'll put your name on the cover in a smaller font," I told him, adding, "I'll give you a piece of the advance and a piece of the royalties."

Jeffrey drove a hard bargain, and I ended up giving over more than I intended to. After I made the deal with him—I had immediate regrets. I gave away much of the advance to Jeffrey, but I needed his hands-on help. I went to New York, where Wiley provided Jeffrey and me with an office to write our book.

When I re-submitted the revised version, Wiley did not request one single change. Hooking up with Jeffrey Leeson was the best move I made in seeing *When the Headline Is You* come to life.

Here's Annie and me in the Barnes & Noble on 5th Avenue in New York.

Annie and Jeff in Barnes & Noble

Before I wrote When the Headline Is You, *I walked into Chapters Indigo, a prominent Canadian bookstore chain. I asked a clerk if they had* When the Headline Is You *by Jeff Ansell.*

I immediately felt embarrassed. Of course, they didn't have the book.

At that point, it hadn't even been written yet. I just wanted a taste of what it feels like to walk into a bookstore and ask for your own book.

Pass the Upside-Down Ketchup Please...

Although *When the Headline Is You* sold well, it wasn't about to make me millions. My ketchup bottle was going to make me rich.

Think back to the early 2000s and the way Heinz Foods used to package its ketchup. If you recall, the bottle stood right side up, making it difficult to empty all the contents inside, and it would leave a layer of residue on the bottom of the bottle. Plus, the dispensing nozzle was always gunky-looking.

Well, my brother-in-law Paul and I came up with the answer to the problem. It hit me when I walked into Paul's bathroom and saw his shampoo and conditioner bottles turned upside down, so they were standing on their caps.

Looking into his fridge, I saw he did the same with his ketchup bottle. The bottle was upside down, almost empty and as clean as can be. You see, unlike the existing packaging, upside-down bottles truly emptied to the last drop—leaving zero residue in the bottle. We can thank gravity for that. Paul was onto something.

We decided we would obtain a patent to produce the bottle and then licence the product to Heinz, Kraft, Nestlé, and any other large company that sold viscous products like mustards, sauces, and even cremes and lotions.

So, we hired a product engineer to design the bottle plus a nozzle that was placed on the bottom end of the container, off to the side so that the nozzle itself never touched the surface it was placed on. That would keep the tabletop or kitchen counter clean.

We poured a fair bit of dough into the container and we developed a prototype bottle. We called it the *Updown* bottle.

The logo (or lettering)—Paul's idea—was brilliant. It was *updn*. Turn the bottle upside down or right side up and it still read *updn*.

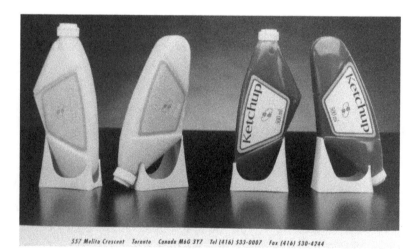

557 Melita Crescent   Toronto   Canada M6G 3Y7   Tel (416) 533-0007   Fax (416) 530-4244

Prototypes for the Updown bottle

I was already counting the royalties, figuring we'd make millions while we slept.

We pitched all the big food companies, including those I mentioned, plus President's Choice, which had an international presence through its generic brands division, selling to Walmart, for instance.

Paul and I were then invited to deliver a fifteen-minute presentation to Dave Nichol, the high-powered and hard-to-pin-down boss of President's Choice. We were all set with a presentation highlighting the merits of our bottle.

In preparing for the presentation, we had two ketchup bottles that had been emptied. One was a President's Choice bottle, and the other was our prototype. The President's Choice bottle looked unappetizing—full of old ketchup residue at the bottom that wouldn't come out, while dried-up ketchup lined the dispensing nozzle. Our bottle, on the other hand, was spotless—clean as a whistle.

When Nichol blew into the room, he told us we had fifteen seconds to make our pitch, not fifteen minutes as promised.

"Mr. Nichol, I only need five seconds," I responded.

I grabbed hold of the President's Choice ketchup and said, "Here's your bottle."

Then I picked up our prototype and said, "Here's our bottle."

Following that "detailed" presentation, I placed both bottles on the table. Enough said.

Though Nichol took a pass, Heinz took our design, tweaked it a bit, and secured their own patents for an upside-down bottle.

We coulda been a player in the bottle business! Coulda, shoulda, woulda.

Would You Believe...

I went to India for a day.

A client with global operations asked if I could do a couple of days of training in Beijing. "Sure," I said. I had never been to Beijing, and it would no doubt be quite the experience. To get to China, I flew over the Pacific.

"On your way home from Beijing, it would be great if you could stop by Mumbai to do some training for our key people there," said my client.

India?

I once jokingly told Annie that because of my finicky stomach, if I ever go to India, I'd survive on peanut butter, Melba toast, Mars bars, and Coke. Indian food may be loved worldwide—but not by me.

Still—what an opportunity, I thought. "Sure, I'll do it!"

Beijing to Mumbai—how far apart could they be? Like New York to Chicago, I figured. Not quite.

Before taking off from Toronto, I made sure I packed Melba toast, a jar of peanut butter, and loads of Mars bars. The trip from Beijing to Mumbai took eighteen hours, including a five-hour stopover in Singapore. I arrived in Mumbai around 2 a.m.

Outside the airport terminal, there were five-year-old children tugging at my pant leg begging for American dollar bills—in the middle of the night. As my taxi drove the streets of Mumbai to get to my hotel, I saw a sample of the profound poverty plaguing the city.

Then, when I got to the Marriott, it was one of the most beautiful hotel rooms I had ever stayed in. It even had steps in it. Yet, when I looked out the window of my hotel room, I mostly saw metal shanties—the irony.

By now, it was 3 a.m. and I needed to be up for work by 6:30.

The training session itself went very well. We started at eight in the morning, but we were still at it by nine in the evening. "Don't these people want to go home?" I thought. By now, I was exhausted, but they were determined to squeeze every bit of learning out of me that they could.

We did take a short lunch and dinner break. Take one guess what I had for each meal.

When I got back to my room around 10 p.m., I set the alarm for 3 a.m. to be in time for my 5 a.m. flight to Frankfurt.

As I later sat at the Mumbai Airport, I might as well have been on the moon. Never in my life had I felt so alone, so far away from home.

To get to China, I flew over the Pacific, and to fly home from India, I flew over the Atlantic. Around the world—literally—in less than seven days.

I wish I had paid more attention in world geography class.

Aloha—Oh No!...

Would you believe I traveled 7,400 km (4,600 miles) to Maui only to discover I brought the wrong training videos with me?

I was ten minutes away from kicking off a crisis communications training program for fourteen executives of a global hotel chain when I realized I'd mistakenly left specially-produced videos for the program on my desk at home, thousands of miles away. Those videos were supposed to carry me through an eight-hour training day. I was screwed. Those videos were integral to the training program.

Also, part of the issue was that the paper handouts I was about to distribute referred to "the video you've just seen." Only there were no videos.

I tried to remain calm.

Getting the videos online wasn't an option at the time. So, what do I do? I quickly scanned my options. I couldn't get the videos couriered in time—I was in Hawaii. That could take at least forty-eight hours. I had less than ten minutes.

Another option was to tell the truth—that I brought the wrong training videos. However, if I did that, the executives would likely feel short-changed and might look for flaws or gaps in the training.

People were starting to walk into the room. It was five minutes to nine.

I had no choice. I didn't have the videos, but I had to deliver the program anyway. I decided the best thing to do was to just barrel ahead as if nothing was wrong.

As I read the phase one paper handout aloud, I improvised by saying, "*Imagine* you've just seen a video that reveals weaknesses in your safety systems." I simply had them picture in their minds what they would have seen on the videos.

As I read the handout, I glanced around the room to see if any of the participants were looking around, wondering about this video (or just looking at me funny). No one was.

My plan worked!

Who—Me?...

I'll always remember how a newspaper headline had me almost fly off my treadmill one morning.

A front-page, above-the-fold headline in the *Toronto Star* referred to the Ontario Liberal Party's secret weapon in the upcoming provincial election to elect Lyn McLeod premier. Oh, this is interesting, I thought. Who or what could their secret weapon be?

I read the article and stopped when the secret weapon was identified as—holy cow—Jeff Ansell!

But it wasn't true. I wasn't a secret weapon for the Liberals. Yes, I had done some work with McLeod prior to the election, but to call me a secret weapon was just not accurate. My role was very modest.

In addition, some people would suspect me of planting the story to glorify myself. There's no way I would do that. If Lyn McLeod won and became premier, I might get some of the credit. But if Lyn McLeod imploded—I risked taking a big bite of a you-know-what sandwich. Not interested—either way.

Plus, the article would serve to piss off those campaign pros who were genuinely busting their ass to get McLeod elected. (She did not win, by the way.)

Years earlier, while still on the radio, I had another case of *who, me?* One evening, my friend Renée and I were in the studio audience for a taping of the popular CFCF-TV sit-com *Excuse My French.*

Before taping starts for a show like this, a local media personality takes the stage to "warm up" the audience and get them into a laughing mood. On this occasion, the warm-up announcer was Nick Hollinrake, whom I'd been watching on TV and listening to on the radio since I was a kid, lying in my parent's bed.

Prior to the start of taping, Nick told the audience of three hundred, "Good evening everybody, and welcome to tonight's taping of *Excuse My French.* We're going to bring out the stars in a moment, but first, I want to take a moment to introduce a celebrity I'd like you all to meet. He's sitting in our audience tonight."

At that point, I craned my neck and scoured the room, looking to see who he was referring to.

"Ladies and gentlemen—please give a warm round of applause for Jeff Ansell of CFCF Radio."

People applauded. I was stunned. When the crowd started to clap, Renée said, "Stand up, Jeffrey. They're clapping for you!" I got up and waved.

Nick made me feel like a million dollars. I learned something very important from Nick that evening. With just a few words, Nick had validated me and made me feel good about myself. And my friend Renée was there to see it.

Years later, when I learned that Nick Hollinrake passed away, I went to his funeral, remembering how his kindness had meant so much to me.

After I began working as a news anchor, people on the street started to recognize me. The recognition felt good.

One day, I was in a big mall, and a saleswoman looked at me and said, "I know you."

Getting all pumped up and full of myself, I started to say, "Thank you for recognizing me," when she quickly went on to repeat, "I know you," adding, "You work in the shoe store."

Pretty humbling, I must say.

CHAPTER TEN

Getting into Harvard

My dear friend Tim Laing (whom I'd worked with exposing the pill pushers of Parkdale) passed on an invitation he received to a course called Dealing with an Angry Public. The course was offered by the MIT-Harvard Public Disputes Program, affiliated with the Harvard Kennedy School (or John F. Kennedy School of Government).

Tim knew that I had just launched my new business, Jeff Ansell & Associates, and that I needed to get my name out there into the marketplace.

The focus of the course was how best to handle multi-party stakeholder disputes. It provided strategies for corporations, government agencies, and PR companies to deal with contentious issues relating to nuclear waste facilities, proposed developments, environmental impacts, changes in corporate or government policy, and so on.

A hundred or so senior executives from many of the world's largest organizations attended the course, held twice annually in Cambridge, Massachusetts.

The course itself, created and led by Professor Larry Susskind, was highly enlightening. Susskind, a world authority on negotiation and dispute resolution, is also the founder of the Consensus Building Institute, based in Cambridge. CBI is a non-profit that does public and private sector consulting.

CBI often employs the *Mutual Gains Approach*, pioneered by Professor Susskind. The Mutual Gains Approach involves multi-party stakeholders—some wanting to find resolution, and others wanting to sabotage the process.

There are six key tenets to the Mutual Gains Approach:
1. Acknowledge the concerns of the other side
2. Encourage joint fact-finding
3. Offer contingent commitments
4. Act in a trustworthy manner
5. Admit mistakes
6. Share information

This is an excellent and enlightened technique. However, as simple as it sounds, this is a complex formula to recreate. The challenge in a multi-party dispute is to reach an agreement when each side wants its own way and uses social media communications as a weapon.

I attended the Cambridge course with four particular objectives in mind:

Step #1 Enjoy time away with Annie

Step #2 Learn

Step #3 Distribute business cards to solicit new business

Step #4 Become an instructor in the Dealing with an Angry Public program

On day one of the course, Professor Susskind addressed the role of media in multi-party stakeholder disputes. Over the lunch break, I introduced myself to him. "I disagree with what you said earlier about working with the news media," I told him.

Respectfully, he more or less said, "That's interesting," and walked away.

Well, I tried.

Later that afternoon, the topic of dealing with the media came up again. Professor Susskind said, "There's somebody here who disagrees with me. Would you care to speak?"

My heart started beating rapidly. I was afraid that if I didn't make my point properly, I would look like a fool in front of all these smart people. But if I didn't do it, I'd miss the opportunity to achieve a key objective in being there. This was my live audition to get me onto the Harvard Dealing with an Angry Public program as an instructor, with a special focus on media and crisis communications.

A wireless microphone was brought over. "Thank you," I said, accepting the microphone.

"My concern is that, since the media shows only snippets of what is said, and often out of context, they could easily undermine the consensus building process. While mutual gains and consensus building are nice theoretically, they are totally contrary to the needs and demands of the news media. Why?" I continued, "Because getting people to agree on a solution is not sexy. Having them disagree is very sexy. The news media organizations do not like solutions. They like conflict. Solutions get in the way of conflict. For reporters, conflict is what pays for the kids' camp in the summer," I went on to say.

"From a news-reporting perspective, the boilerplate approach to covering angry public issues serves to promote a good-versus-evil dynamic. Angry public stories in the media are generally created by editors and producers who conduct a daily casting call for the news," I said.

"Reporters are encouraged to seek out a predictable cast of characters in their stories, characters sure to include the hero, villain, and incompetent witness and/or expert, preferably dressed in a white lab coat for TV audiences. A reporter will talk to a victim or a perceived 'good guy' in a story and ask questions as if there's a halo above their head, like they're talking to the pope," I stated. "Then, they go to the 'bad guy,' and it's like he's got horns coming out of his head.

"They lend their own perspectives to emphasize the drama and the conflict through the tone, quality, and types of questions they ask. We need to marry the two goals of consensus building and meeting the media's needs in a way that enables all to be true to their values, true to their cause, and true to their supporters—without undermining the objective of mutual gain.

"We need to bear in mind that questions will be framed, phrased, and textured in a way that promotes tension. That's why it's critical we make our values front and center in all we do and all we say—while controlling context—without PR spin," I concluded.

There—I was done. That was my big audition.

At the end of the two-day program, Professor Susskind came over to me. "I like what you had to say. I want you to bring the media component to the next scheduled Dealing with an Angry Public program in six months."

Amazingly, I achieved all four objectives on that initial trip—including a few great days away with Annie.

As excited as I was to now be a part of the program, I was over-whelmed by the idea. This was the Public Disputes Program at Harvard Law School. The best and the brightest study and teach here. I ended up working alongside Larry and fellow instructor Michael Wheeler for fourteen years to deliver the Dealing with an Angry Public course. I learned so much from them.

CEOs, executives, White House and State Department officials, attorneys general, NASA, and senior legal and public affairs executives from every sector—pharmaceutical, automotive, energy, gas, defense, etc.—took the course.

Even a well-known but disgraced TV evangelist attended the course. Peter Popoff was known for, among other things, his jet-black hair, his ability to speak in tongues, and the secret faith tools from Heaven that he sold. On his TV show, Popoff would walk amongst his audience of followers and identify their names and ailments without even asking.

That's because his wife, Liz, was surreptitiously feeding Popoff's hidden earpiece with previously determined info. Popoff was exposed as a fraud on *The Tonight Show*, where Johnny Carson, with the help of magic debunker, the Amazing Randi, revealed Popoff's ruse by actu-ally recording Liz's instructions to her husband.

At the Angry Public course, Popoff and his daughter approached me. "We'd like to hire you. What's your daily rate?" I named an outra-geous fee simply because I didn't want the gig. Not even me or the "Dealing with an Angry Public" program could help Popoff. Believe it or not though, Peter Popoff still remains on late-night TV in markets across North America.

Nerves were always a factor for me in delivering my portion of the

Angry Public program, especially because of the dramatic way I made my entrance.

Attendees of the course would be working on a case study involving a pharmaceutical drug believed to be responsible for several deaths. As the reporter, I would be privy to information that the audience as a whole did not know. My job was to ambush them and to focus on the conflict between the parties to get them to give me the juiciest story or quotes that I could get.

At a designated point during the course, I would barge into the conference hall, shine the bright lights of my camera on an unsuspecting audience member, almost blinding them, and hit them with a barrage of nasty questions.

"I'm Jeff Ansell from N-E-W-S. Why are you letting people suffer? How many people have to die before you'll take action? Why are you covering this up?"

After grilling the person who's been playing the role of company CEO, I would then face the camera to do my stand-up. "There you have it. The president of this besieged company refusing to take responsibility for the deaths of countless Americans. I'm Jeff Ansell, N-E-W-S."

The room would erupt in applause.

Most reporters don't go into interviews consciously trying to break parties apart. Clearly, in the Angry Public program, I try to represent an extreme in my interviews so as to prepare executives for the toughest encounters they might face. But afterward, one of the first questions I ask is, "Has anybody in this room ever experienced that?" About half of them will raise their hands. So, it's not as far out there as one might imagine.

That was on day one of the program. On day two, I provided context and perspective surrounding relationships with an angry public. However, the problem was that on day one, I scared the pants off people with my aggressive approach, which was designed to throw them off-kilter. On day two, they were afraid to talk to me—for fear I would pounce on them. They were afraid to even look at me.

So, I would start off my talk on the second day by saying, "Ladies and Gentlemen, I won't be doing any hard-hitting interviews today, so it's okay to have eye contact with me." They laughed.

Then I said, "Sometimes when I deliver the Dealing with an Angry Public program, I feel as popular as a pig at a bar mitzvah." They laughed again.

And then, I went into dealing with an angry public.

Feeling Intimidated...

Each time I reflect on my Harvard experience, I feel humbled and grateful. I also think to myself that it's something my parents would have gotten a kick out of. Their high school dropout son was now an instructor at Harvard!

Still, who was I to teach such a high-powered crowd? After all, I've had many a moment where you can swim in my deepest thoughts and not get your ankles wet. I would call myself "moderately intelligent" most of the time, as opposed to "overly bright," but that by itself didn't get me into Harvard.

So, how did I get in? What am I doing as an instructor at Harvard Law School? I know that something more got me to Harvard—I just don't know what or why.

No doubt, the divine hand played a key part in it. After all, I didn't even finish high school, for heaven's sake.

Even though I created my own content, I never felt 100% comfortable as an instructor in the Dealing with an Angry Public program. I often had the jitters in the days leading up to it. There were so many bigshots taking the course—people at the top of their field, especially from the world of PR—it only intimidated me more. Besides, only delivering the program twice a year prevented an opportunity to bullet-proof and hone my presentation in front of audiences.

The night before one of the programs, I was woken up by a call to my hotel room. It was from a key competitor of mine, with whom I wasn't particularly close or friendly. "Jeff, I'm in Cambridge and I'm taking your course tomorrow and Friday," he told me.

Like I wasn't feeling enough pressure—now my key competition was going to be in the crowd, no doubt to make mischief or somehow throw me off my game.

Up early the next morning, with "that feeling" in the pit of my stomach, I had breakfast and hoped I could keep it down. As I walked toward the conference hall, my heart started to beat faster and faster.

I got through the first day of the program okay, though I still felt off-balance because of the presence of my competitor. On the final day of the program, we introduced a scenario involving a group of people who were angry at the actions of a fictional corporation.

A name was drawn out of a hat for someone to play the part of the corporate spokesperson. Wouldn't you know it—my competitor's name was selected. I could tell he was nervous when he came up to the front of the room. My job was to rattle him into saying something totally inappropriate.

One part of me wanted to tie him up in word knots. But I could see he was already on edge, and the Higher Self in me decided on another approach. I worked to make him look good.

He knew it too. Though we never talked about it, after the program, our entire relationship changed. I'm pleased to say he's now a trusted friend.

Lecturing Harvard MBAs...

Shortly after I became an instructor in the Dealing with an Angry Public program as part of Harvard Law School, I was invited to lecture at Harvard Business School.

Professor Mike Wheeler, with whom I did the Dealing with an Angry Public program (with Professor Susskind), brought me in to lecture his MBA students in the Harvard Business School Program on Negotiation. For twenty straight years, Mike and his colleagues Andrew Wasynczuk, Brian Hall, and John Beshears invited me to help teach a class on Negotiating Complex Deals and Disputes.

It's a lot of fun working with MBA students at Harvard. As the CEOs and government leaders of tomorrow, aside from the occasional know-it-all and pissant, the Harvard students were eager to learn. Coming from all over the world, the MBA students were very challenging—as they are taught and should be. I enjoyed the opportunity to exchange ideas with them early in their careers.

MBA students generally are so busy learning about finance, operations, marketing, human resources, management, and everything else that goes into running a company, that it's easy to forget what a higher purpose in their learning might be.

"When you're engaged in a public policy dispute, let your values lead the way," I told each class. "Identify the values at play in any given situation and ask yourself the question: What's the right thing to do? Money aside—PR spin aside—what's the right thing to do? Then, providing they're consistent with your values, apply your learnings from Harvard."

One class that I participated in involved a case study of the Deepwater Horizon BP oil spill. In my consulting practice, I worked on this disaster on behalf of Anadarko, one of BP's partners in the project.

The MBA students were playing the roles of BP's CEO and general counsel. In our exercise, they were preparing to meet with President Obama in what was expected to be a stressful discussion over BP's obligations to the nation resulting from the environmental disaster.

I observed their preparations for the "Oval Office" meeting and then discussed why their entire approach was misguided.

It was too defensive.

The Erin Brockovich Case...

The Dealing with an Angry Public program led me to the Erin Brockovich case.

A senior executive of the PG&E Corporation approached me at one of our Harvard programs. "I would like you to review an ABC News report about water we allegedly contaminated in Hinkley, California." Pacific Gas & Electric (a PG&E division) was blamed for poisoning Hinkley's water from 1952 to 1966.

"We're accused of having high quantities of a chemical called hexavalent chromium in the town's water supply." Hexavalent chromium, also known as Chromium-6, was used in the cooling system of the nearby compressor station.

The Hinkley drinking water supply had been contaminated with 1,400 million liters (320 million gallons) of chromium-tainted wastewater. Evidence indicated a great many diseases prevalent in the community, dating back to the '60s, '70s, and '80s—cancer, leukemia, birth defects, Hodgkin's disease—at rates higher than national averages. PG&E was vilified, and rightly so.

The community was being rallied by Erin Brockovich, a lawyer's assistant in California who organized a major legal action against PG&E. Actress Julia Roberts played Erin in the movie named after the film's hero.

I prepared a multi-page report for PG&E of what I thought the company had done wrong in its communications with the community, stakeholders, the public, and the media. PG&E was highly untrustworthy. For instance, the search for documents highlighting the results of water tests were missing. They were likely destroyed amid allegations of a PG&E coverup.

Company spokespeople showed no empathy for the people of Hinkley, whose lives had been devastated by PG&E.

I was invited to San Francisco to meet with the company CEO. With my avenging reporter background, it would have been easy for me to see PG&E as "the enemy." But I wasn't a reporter anymore, and this was how I now earned my living.

Plus, the fact I was invited to San Francisco helped me see PG&E as a company that wanted to make a change. Faced with the largest civil lawsuit in US history, plus a potential PR nightmare, I could sense that PG&E now wanted to do what was right.

When we learned about the *Erin Brockovich* movie featuring a major Hollywood star, we needed to prepare for the fallout. I began media training their most senior executives and spokespeople.

My internal message to PG&E in this PR battle was that the company didn't deserve to win. We were on the wrong side of right. After all, the story is true—it did happen. There was no point in being defensive anymore.

So, PG&E strengthened environmental policies and practices while we created and delivered messages, largely ones of admission, contrition, and action. PG&E was finally acknowledging the concerns of the other side and it settled with the community for $333 million, the largest amount ever in a civil action in the United States.

The movie went on to become one of the biggest hits of the year. Remarkably, it triggered no new public outcry against PG&E. Today, Hinkley is described as a ghost town.

Following my many years of work with PG&E, I received an email from Greg Pruett, formerly senior vice president of the company. Greg said it was a fortuitous day for PG&E when we met at Harvard's Kennedy School of Government. Amongst his kind words of my positive impact on the employees, customers, and leadership through sharing my strategies to be a compassionate communicator, he said it was the focus on doing what is right that made the biggest impact.

The FBI Director, Me, and the Bomb Detector...

The Dealing with an Angry Public program also led me to work with international law enforcement.

The world of policing is rapidly changing. On a local level, police forces are dealing with a wide number of issues that have created angry stakeholders. Riots have erupted in major cities, mostly in the United States. "Defund the police" and "end systemic racism" are frequent calls from critics. What makes these concerns even more pressing is the presence of camera phones on hand to capture police-civilian encounters for YouTube.

On a larger scale, globally-sized issues have emerged for international law enforcement, including cybercrime, money laundering, drug cartels, and of course, terrorism.

Over the years, I've done a great deal of work with local police services, as well as for law enforcement at every level, including the FBI, US Secret Service, RCMP, and police chiefs from around the world through the International Association of Chiefs of Police (IACP).

The IACP, based in Alexandria, Virginia, just outside of Washington, had engaged me several times to coach their leadership. I was especially honored when they invited me to speak at their 2015 IACP Conference in Chicago. Another of their speakers, the next day, was President Obama.

I was doubly honored when the IACP asked me to moderate the first-ever public gathering of the Five Eyes, which included the FBI director at the time, James Comey. The Five Eyes is an intelligence alliance made up of the United States (FBI/CIA), Canada (RCMP/CSIS), United Kingdom (National Crime Agency), and Australian and New Zealand Police.

The relationship among the Five Eyes is said to be one of the most comprehensive espionage alliances in history—dating back to the time of Winston Churchill.

> *The Five Eyes hasn't been without controversy.*
>
> *Former NSA contractor Edward Snowden described the Five Eyes as a "supra-national intelligence organization that does not answer to the known laws of its own countries."*

I jumped at the opportunity to chair a panel discussion with Jim Comey and, literally, the English-speaking world's top criminal investigators.

But en route from Toronto to Chicago, I was apprehended by US customs agents who suspected I was carrying a bomb. Not a good start to a trip to meet the director of the FBI!

Here's what happened. The day before I was scheduled to fly into Chicago, I went to a medical clinic to have a nuclear stress test. In order to conduct the test, a radioactive dye was injected into my body.

I knew from previous experience that when a person going through airport security has very recently been injected with radioactive dye, it will set off the agents' beepers and alarms. So, I made sure to get a letter from the medical clinic attesting to the fact I'd just had the radioactive injection. However, there wasn't enough time at US customs to let them know.

As I stood in line to hand over my paperwork to the agent—the radiation beepers went off. "Freeze, everyone!" shouted the agent. "It's me—I set off the alarm," I yelled out, clutching the doctor's letter. "Here's the medical letter to explain."

I tried to hand the letter to the customs person, but quickly found myself surrounded by five agents who hustled me into secondary—where travelers are brought when there's something suspicious about them.

Once inside, I presented my doctor's letter, which, after about thirty anxious minutes, they confirmed as valid. Then, they wanted to know why I was traveling to the United States. I suspected that if I told them I was going to meet with the director of the FBI, I'd find myself in handcuffs in a New York minute. So, I mentioned the fact I was speaking at a Chicago conference.

When they asked for my US visa to allow me to enter the country for this event (I didn't have one), I told the agents I would be speaking for free. That way—no visa required. They let me through.

My speech in front of two thousand federal, state, and local police officials went well. It was the Five Eyes panel discussion that worried me—and literally kept me up all night.

Before the big event, I made sure to arrive ninety-minutes early in the convention hall to ensure the panel was set up was to my satisfaction. It wasn't. There was a problem with the layout of the dais. It was small to begin with, and we needed enough room for the Five Eyes and me, plus a podium.

Organizers of the event had planned for Comey to sit at a distant end of the table. But that would have meant all six-feet-eight-inches of him would have needed to dipsy-doodle his way past five of us on a riser that was already too tiny. It would have been embarrassing for him, and highly uncomfortable for the audience if Comey were to fall off the stage.

After I rearranged the seating chart (me in the middle, with Comey closest to the podium), his FBI bodyguards swept in.

"Everybody is to leave the conference hall, now," demanded Comey's security detail. As we did so, the Four (other) Eyes were less than pleased. In fact, the order to exit the room truly pissed off Bob Paulson, commissioner of the RCMP. "Does Jim know about this?" snapped Paulson.

Then, they brought in the dogs to sniff for bombs. Good thing I was ushered out of the hall earlier, in case I was still giving off that radioactive scent.

When Comey arrived, he and I spent a few private moments chatting as we ate our box lunches. In our conversation, the director was easy to be with, friendly, and humble.

"Director Comey, I'd like to review your bio with you to ensure you're pleased with how I introduce you. Here's what I'm going to say—'James Comey, seventh director of the US Federal Bureau of Investigation was born in Yonkers, New York...'"

"You can stop there—that's fine," Comey said.

"I can't stop there—I need to say more about you." Together, director Comey and I bounced a few more sentences around until we had the introduction nailed.[24]

Former FBI Director James Comey & Jeff

As I said, I found Comey likable. In fact, as the Five Eyes and I sat on the panel waiting for the event to start, Comey said, "So, Jeff—tell us more about yourself and what you do."

Truth is, I was flustered. What do I tell him? That I'm a media and speech advisor? If I said that, it might sound like I was pitching them for business, and I didn't want to give off that impression.

I didn't know what to say. Winging it and trying desperately to impress Comey and the others, I said, "I used to be an investigative journalist who caught two Nazi war criminals." Comey nodded politely, as did the others, and the event went off flawlessly.

I should have mentioned (but forgot to) that much of my Nazi investigation relied on the US Justice Department, since Comey, after all, was formerly deputy attorney general of the United States.

CHAPTER ELEVEN
Political Encounters

Though I've met several Canadian prime ministers, two of them stand out—one for trying to choke me, the other for having his security man elbow me in the gut.

Years ago, when he was confronted by a loud and angry protestor, Jean Chrétien gave the disgruntled man the now-famous "Shawinigan handshake." Chrétien, from the town of Shawinigan, Quebec, grabbed the protestor by the throat and squeezed his neck. That came to be known as the Shawinigan handshake.

I was most mindful of the handshake when I had the opportunity to say hello to Chrétien at an Ottawa event honoring the governor general of Canada. When I reached out my hand to shake his—you guessed it—Chretien ignored my hand and gave me the famous neck grab. Wrapping his fingers around my neck, he said in that gravelly voice of his, "Shawinigan handshake!"

Why did he do it? Chrétien's eyes were glassy and he appeared tipsy. That may be why. Still, I was truly honored that I warranted the Shawinigan handshake!

Prime Minister Jean Chrétien & Jeff

Covering elections was a part of my job, so when Brian Mulroney was running to be re-elected prime minister of Canada, I was assigned to follow him around in case he made news.

On one particular day, Mulroney appointed a woman named Doris Lau to be a citizenship court judge. Lau, a prominent member of the Conservative party, was accused of being a patronage appointment and there was a public outcry. My role that day was to get the prime minister to comment on the controversy.

As he disembarked from his campaign bus, I shouted, "Prime Minister, would you comment on the Doris Lau scandal?" Mulroney ignored me. As he walked along, I shouted the question again—no response.

When I asked a third time, an RCMP bodyguard shoved his elbow into my stomach. It hurt. I doubled over.

Later, as Mulroney was walking back to the campaign bus to prepare for his next stop, I shouted out one last time—"Prime Minister, will you answer my question?" to which Mulroney finally looked at me and replied, "Not if it's the same question you've been asking all day!"

It's a good thing Mulroney took action against Nazis by creating the Deschênes Commission of Inquiry on War Criminals in Canada. Otherwise, he would be on my shit list, like Trudeau #1.

This Guy Has All the Parts—I Thought...

In 2004, a Chicago-based client introduced me to a friend of his who aspired to represent Illinois in the US Senate. His friend was Republican Jack Ryan, and he wanted me to play a role in his upcoming Senate campaign.

On paper and in person, Jack was the perfect candidate. A former Wall Street investment banker with tens of millions of dollars, Jack had cashed out to become a teacher in a rough Chicago neighborhood.

I flew into Chicago to meet Jack over dinner at the O'Hare Hilton. He was Kennedyesque in appearance, and by the end of dessert I was convinced he had the parts to go the distance to beat his Democratic rival for the senate, who Jack referred to as a relative "unknown."

Jack had gone to Dartmouth and obtained an MBA, plus a law degree from Harvard. (Did I mention I was an instructor there?) Following university, Jack worked at a refugee camp for Latinos fleeing the Central American civil wars.

"I stand for tax cuts, reduced federal spending, and equal opportunity in education," Jack told me.

"Jack, are there any skeletons in your closet?" I asked.

"No," he answered.

"I need to know, Jack—is there anything in your background that could be used against you?"

"Absolutely not," he insisted.

At that point, I had visions of counseling Jack in the Oval Office. We agreed to work together on his Senate campaign.

Shortly after I met Jack for dinner that night, the truth came out.

Unsealed court documents alleged Jack pressured his ex-wife to perform sexual acts in public. Jack never told me his ex-wife was actress Jeri Ryan, who appeared on TV's *Star Trek, Law and Order,* and *NCIS.*

Jack was forced to give up his campaign.

The Democrat "unknown" went on to win the Illinois senate race. His name: Barack Obama. The rest, as they say, is quite literally, history.

A Plan to Meet Bill Clinton...

President Clinton was coming to town to speak at a fundraising event organized by a group called the Society for Yad Vashem.

Yad Vashem is the name of the Holocaust memorial in Jerusalem. The society helps promote public education about the Holocaust and stands for tolerance in the community worldwide.

I, of course, had spent a year devoted to hunting Nazis.

I ordered tickets for the president's speech and dinner to follow. I knew right away that if the former president was coming to town, I wanted to meet him.

Beyond that, I didn't really have a plan to meet Mr. Clinton. I just knew I had to come up with one. Using a four-step plan—this time, with the end in mind—I started off by working backward:

Step #4 Personally meet President Clinton

Step #3 Offer to write the speech that introduces the president

Step #2 Set up a meeting with Yad Vashem event organizers

Step #1 Buy tickets to the event

Now that I had the backward steps identified to achieve my ultimate goal to meet President Clinton, I needed to turn it into an action plan going forward.

Step #1 Buy tickets to the event

If, for some reason, my plan wouldn't materialize, at least Annie and I would get to attend the president's speech.

Step #2 Set up a meeting with Yad Vashem event organizers

Remember, you don't get if you don't ask.

I contacted the group's executive director and said, "My name is Jeff Ansell. I am a media, crisis, and speech adviser for people at very high levels. Additionally, I've been an investigative journalist who hunted and caught two Nazi war criminals."

It was my way of saying (in fifteen seconds), "I'm not a nutcase."

Step #3 Offer to write the speech that introduces the president

I would research Clinton's ties to Holocaust-related events and subject matter to help me write the speech. For added value (if needed), I'd also offer to train their spokespeople prior to the event.

Step #4 Personally meet President Clinton

President Bill Clinton & Jeff

The plan was successful.

When President Clinton walked into the VIP reception prior to the evening's events—he looked larger than life.

"Mr. President, I'm Jeff Ansell. This is my wife, Annie Ansell."

"Nice to meet you," he said to each of us.

Getting into position for a picture on either side of the president, Annie and I put our hands around him, and then he put his arms around us. As we're standing there posing, I began talking to him.

"Mr. President, I'd be honored, sir, if you would sign a book we brought." The book was called *The Clinton Years* by Robert McNeely, which is a pictorial essay of his presidency.

"I love this book," the president said. "It's one of my favorites."

"Mr. President, we have some people in common." I mentioned Craig Smith, his former political director at the White House, and Howard Paster, my old boss at Hill and Knowlton worldwide. Howard was Clinton's chief liaison to Congress.

"Great. Well, say hello to those fellows if you see them before I do," he said.

"I will."

About an hour later, Annie and I were standing in the foyer, waiting to go into the ballroom for the big dinner. When the presidential entourage arrived, in came Mr. Clinton, three Secret Service Agents, two RCMP officers, and a couple of members of his personal staff.

Walking right in front of us, the president stopped, went up to Annie and said in that slow Arkansan southern drawl, "We meet again, Annie."

She was blown away. The president of the United States remembered her name!

Next, he turned to me, gave me a smile, and said, "So, Jeff—tell me more about what you do."

"Mr. President, my role as a media counselor is to advise people in tough, high-profile, no-win situations."

"Well, I've had a few of those," chuckled the president.

Clinton then looked me straight in the eyes, holding his gaze on me for about three or so seconds.

I looked back and held my eyes on him for just as long.

Thoughts flashed through my head.

Should I give him my card?

This is my best moment.

Will he ever call?

I doubt it.

But I'll never know if I don't give it to him.

Having already prepared, I had my business card ready to go, and on the back, I'd written a personal note with my home phone number.

He took my card into the palm of his hand, nodded, put it into his pocket, shook my hand again, and moved on.

> *Prior to the event, I trained a benefactor who, in our practice sessions, was a terrible speaker. Not only that, but he also came across as highly arrogant.*
>
> *Though he was born on third base, he was convinced he'd hit a triple. He was lucky his father had a PhD—his papa had dough. He acted as if I was his manservant, at his beck and call. He was rude to my staff too.*
>
> *I was working with him for free here, so I felt at liberty to tell him, "You're not very likable, you know."*
>
> *"I don't care," was his response.*
>
> *"Let's watch the video I just made of you reading your intro to the president. I'm going to play it back with no sound. Just look at the guy speaking—forget it's you—and tell me if you're interested in hearing what he has to say."*
>
> *I rolled the video.*
>
> *"How interested are you in hearing what he has to say?"*
>
> *"So-so."*
>
> *"How likable do you think that fellow is we're looking at?"*
>
> *"Not very," he admitted hesitantly.*
>
> *That was a turning point for us. In fact, the benefactor (whose speech I wrote) was personally congratulated by the president for his*

captivating delivery and meaningful content.

He later sent me a beautiful gift basket to show his appreciation.

Classy.

Richard Nixon Charmed Annie...

On the subject of US presidents...

Annie and I were in Key Biscayne, Florida, having breakfast in our hotel restaurant. Our waiter told us we'd just missed seeing former President Nixon having breakfast with his buddy Bebe Rebozo. Bummer, I thought.

Later, I returned to our room while Annie shopped for a bathing suit downstairs. When she came back up to the room, she was excited and out of breath.

"You'll never guess who I just had a long conversation with!"

"Paul McCartney?" I guessed.

"No, Richard Nixon!" exclaimed Annie. "He was so nice. We talked about Toronto. We talked about the Blue Jays. He was such a gentleman and so charming."

So, there you go.

Rocking in President Kennedy's Chair...

On a visit to Waltham, Massachusetts, I met with Dave Powers, considered one of President John F. Kennedy's closest friends. Though he had an official White House title, Powers was the fellow JFK turned to when he needed time to relax with a buddy.

In later years, Dave became the museum curator of the Kennedy Library. Prior to that, he spent years collecting JFK records, documents, mementos, memorabilia, presidential furniture, and such, and stored it in the Federal Record Center at the National Archives in Waltham.

When I was a reporter, Dave invited me to visit the center and led me to President Kennedy's famous rocking chair, designed by the musculoskeletal pain expert who was President Kennedy's personal physician. Because of his bad back, the president was most comfortable in the rocking chair during meetings.[25]

Seeing me eyeing the chair, Dave asked if I wanted to sit in it, as President Kennedy had done hundreds of times.

I did. I rocked in it. It was quite the rush.

President Bush's Handshake...

I was invited to be one of two platform speakers at a convention of the International Cemetery, Cremation & Funeral Association in Houston, Texas.

A day before my trip, I discovered the other speaker was former President George H. W. Bush. I almost fell off my chair. My anxiety was off the chart. Never before had I shared a stage with an American president. I was nervous.

I was also concerned that President Bush and I could have a meaningful chat in our private time together before the speeches, hopefully without awkward pauses in conversation. So, I bought his book, *A World Transformed*, to read on my flight over.

Worse comes to worst, I figured I'd bring up a story or two from the book that clearly meant something important to him. For instance, the time he sent his son and grandson to Turkey to help earthquake victims.

When I was introduced to President Bush, we shook hands—only it wasn't a normal handshake. As soon as our palms made contact, President Bush sharply flipped my hand over so that his hand was planted on top of mine—clearly demonstrating his dominance in our encounter.

That really wasn't necessary—of course he was the dominant one—he was the president! He actually caused my wrist some discomfort.

George H. W. Bush & Jeff

I told the president I was looking forward to his keynote because I thought he was a fine public speaker. "No, not really," said the president. "I've never been a good public speaker."

That really took me aback. Here's a president of the United States denigrating his speaking skills in a private conversation with me.

Wow.

Panic Attack with the President Nearby...

Ever hear the expression that sometimes the worst thing that happens to you turns out to be the best thing that happens to you? The moment in question took place in Houston, that day with the president.

I didn't tell President Bush about my own struggles with public speaking, which later that day came back with a dark vengeance.

After my handful of live, on-the-air panic attacks, I learned how to breathe properly, and the problem went away—but not for good.

Now, a little nervousness is fine and natural. After all, it's okay to have butterflies, as long as the butterflies are flying in formation.

I was about to follow a former president on stage, and there were several thousand people in the audience. As I stood backstage waiting in the wings while President Bush wrapped up, my anxiety kicked in and rapidly went into high gear.

Then, I felt something grab my ankles. The shark was back. The same shark that tried to swallow me on live TV and radio.

This was the worst possible time for the shark to return. I was about to take the stage with a president of the United States, and I was truly petrified. I tried desperately to practice what I preach.

As I recounted in my LinkedIn Learning video course, *Communicating with Confidence*, I realized I had been holding my breath. So, I said to myself: "Okay, Jeff—pretend you're with a client who is having a meltdown. What's the first thing you would tell them?"

Breathe.

So, I started to breathe. I felt the shark loosen her grip. By then, I asked myself what words describe how I want to come across. Words like insightful, engaging, entertaining, and humorous came to mind.

By focusing on that instead of "oh shit—I hope I don't screw up," I pre-determined a positive outcome. The shark's grip weakened. She still had me trapped, though I did feel my heart slow.

Making Fake Confidence Real in Five Seconds...

Just as I was about to go on stage, I saw my hands were shaking—and that's a tell for sure. I can't let anyone see my hands nervously shake because I'm supposed to be good at this. So, I needed to find a way to cover up my anxiety, not to mention my trembling hands. And I'm grateful to say, I found the answer.

I did something that day that changed my life as a speaker forever— I learned how to turn fake confidence into genuine confidence in a matter of seconds.

My hands and arms did it for me.

As I walked on stage, I said, "Good morning, everyone," using firm hand gestures. "Thank you so much for inviting me to be here today. Mr. President—it's an honor to share the stage.

"President Bush spoke about life in the White House, and I want to talk about life in the glare of the media spotlight." By that point, only seconds later, I had confidence—real confidence, not fake confidence.

You see, when we're genuinely confident, hormones like endorphins and dopamine give us strong body language and conviction in our voice. So, if genuine confidence helps us look strong, I discovered that day that *looking* strong can give us genuine confidence. Using my hands and arms in strong, bold gestures helped my brain believe I was genuinely confident.

Instead of entering the house of confidence by way of the front door, I climbed in through the side window.

Regardless of how I got there, I was in the house.

I'm very happy to say that my Houston presentation went on to be one of the best talks I ever gave.

Bush-Cheney 2004 Campaign...

Though I, as yet, have not had the opportunity to shake the hand of President George W. Bush to test out its mettle, I did have the chance to work for the Bush-Cheney 2004 presidential campaign.

My contact came through the work I had done on the Erin Brockovich case. A senior PG&E official I trained to talk about the Brockovich case became communications director in the Bush White House.

My contact was Nicolle Wallace, commentator on the *Today Show*. Briefly, my four-step plan:

Step #1 Re-establish contact with Nicolle

Step #2 Because foreign nationals are not allowed to be paid in US presidential campaigns, offer to do the gig for free—just for the experience of coaching in the big leagues

Step #3 Make it easy for the Bush-Cheney campaign to engage me, by booking my own hotel and travel

Step #4 Travel to Washington to conduct the training

Nicolle invited me to the Republican National Headquarters in DC to media train her, the chief campaign strategist Matthew Dowd (now an *ABC News* political analyst), the deputy campaign manager Mark Wallace, and Governor Marc Racicot of Montana, who was the chairman of the Republican National Committee.

I was totally blown away by the studio technology at RNC headquarters. They had actual TV studios and news sets to really set the scene for our work together.

As part of our work together, we identified worst-case scenarios to be prepared for, like another 9/11. We also rehearsed a mid-campaign terror attack, which, in our scenario, killed three thousand US troops. Rehearsing responses to another terrorist attack was jolting.

By the way, Nicolle went on to be the chief handler for Sarah Palin, running mate to former presidential candidate John McCain. Nicolle arranged media interviews for Palin, and when Palin began tanking in media interviews, she took it out on Nicolle.

Nicolle later admitted that despite her key role in the McCain-Palin campaign, she didn't even vote.

CHAPTER TWELVE
Celebrity Encounters

When it comes to meeting celebrities, I am quite the fame magnet. I have always had a propensity for meeting famous people quite randomly, like actors John Malkovich and Michael Keaton—each of whom I bumped into and spoke with twice.

I was thirteen years old when the 1968 film *2001: A Space Odyssey* came out. It was shot in widescreen, so the film was playing at the fancy Cinerama Theatre in Montreal, where you booked specific seats at the front wicket.

When my brother-in-law Buzzie bought us two tickets, the wicket lady said, "You'll be excited to hear who you're sitting next to!"

Turns out it was Harry Belafonte—the singer, songwriter, and actor. Belafonte was also a confidant of Reverend Martin Luther King, Jr. Once we took our seats, in walked Belafonte with his wife and two kids, including daughter Shari, who later went on to be famous in her own right.

Too excited to talk to him, I kept to myself.

Halfway through the movie, it was time for intermission (which they had at some theaters in those days). That's when everyone rushes to the bathroom, knowing there will be large line-ups.

As I stood in line to use the urinal, I felt a towering presence standing behind me. I turned around—Harry Belafonte was in the bathroom standing behind me. When it was my turn at the urinal, I was too nervous to go, so I stood there pretending I was taking care of business.

Later, when we were filing out of the theater, I got an autograph.

But I still had to piss like a racehorse—worse than before.

Sneaking In the Back Way...

As promised—the Jerry Seinfeld story.

Adam, my son, was twelve years old when we snuck onto the *Seinfeld* set in Studio City, California.

While visiting Los Angeles, we met up with my friend Kim, who worked in Studio City. Kim's office was directly across the street from Jerry Seinfeld's studio lot bungalow. I had to see the bungalow up close for myself. Sure enough, outside the bungalow, there were two parking spots reserved for Jerry's Porsches.

So, I asked my friend, "Where's Jerry?"

"He's on the set shooting," she said, referring to the huge sound stage, about three hundred feet from where we were standing.

"Well, let's go in!" I said.

"You can't right now," Kim said. "He's very private and he doesn't like people on the set. I could show you the way in, but you can expect to be thrown out and maybe even arrested for trespassing."

With Adam accompanying me, I really didn't want to be tossed out of the studio because then I'd be quite embarrassed in front of him. So, I had to balance my desire to get onto the set with my fear that I was going to lose face in my son's eyes.

In a perfect world, here's how I saw this adventure unfold:

Step #1 Walk over to the studio where Seinfeld *is shot*

Step #2 Get inside the Seinfeld *studio*

Step #3 See the Seinfeld *set*

Step #4 See Jerry himself on the set of Seinfeld
(if he's there) and then quickly leave

Rather than try to walk in through the front door leading us into the *Seinfeld* set, I looked for the back door. Lo and behold, I was able to pry it open.

Adam and I quietly snuck in, careful not to slam the door behind us. We were now standing behind the set of the *Seinfeld* show. Steps 1 and 2 were accomplished.

It was dark back there, and I whispered to Adam, "Shhh, I think I hear something. It's Jerry's voice." I didn't know if Jerry was actually on the other side of the set or whether it was a recording we just heard.

"Let's check it out," I whispered.

Adam and I peeked through a crack in the set, and sure enough, Jerry was there. He was sitting in a director's chair, reading from a script. He was wearing glasses, and at the time, had a cast on his arm. (I didn't get a chance to ask why.)

I softly said to Adam, "Here's what we're going to do. We're going to go left and walk behind the set and then turn right on to the front of the set. As you walk by the front, look to the right and you'll see Jerry's living room and the interior of Monks, the restaurant where they all hang out. Do not stop and stare or saunter along like you're at the carnival. Walk like you have a purpose in being there.

Walk like this." I demonstrated. So, we silently strutted with vigor, determined to look as if we belong there.

"Be sure to breathe, too," I said quietly, finger to lips.

Then, we each took a deep breath, held our heads up high—and walked out determinedly onto the *Seinfeld* set.

Step #3 See the Seinfeld *set*

As we're walking across the set, I'm silently thinking, "Oh, this is Jerry's living room. It's really small in person." Still in my head, "Here's the set for the Monks restaurant. Wow! It looks just like it does on TV."

Step #4 See Jerry himself on the set of Seinfeld *(he was there)*

Up ahead on our left, Jerry, still in the director's chair, was in conversation with someone (might have been Larry David—not sure).

This is where I became really scared because my boy was with me. I didn't want to make an arse out of myself. In that moment, Jerry stopped talking and looked up as if to say, "Who the hell are you?

Who let you in here? And what's that kid doing here???"

My heart was going a mile a minute. I was trying to breathe to stay cool.

As I reached Jerry, I marched by and gave him a firm nod of my head.

Jerry Seinfeld nodded back and watched as Adam and I marched out the front door.

Unbelievably, the plan worked.

Sneaking onto the *Seinfeld* set also reinforced the very real power of non-verbal communication. Body language and facial expression are impactful tools, often more effective than words.

> *Adam and I were in New York on holiday when we took Kramer's Reality Tour. Remember that? Seinfeld even did an episode or two on the tour.*
>
> *In the show, Kramer rents a bus and drives people around New York to show them the landmarks and hangouts in his life—his own bedroom window, the one covered in chicken wire for instance. Well, there's a real Kramer—Kenny Kramer—the inspiration for Michael Richard's character.*
>
> *On the day Adam and I went on the tour, we climbed on the real Kramer's bus, which brought us to a snack bar where we ate Mars bars with knives and forks. Then, we drove by the exterior of Tom's Restaurant, used as the outside of Monk's, the restaurant they're always in.*
>
> *Actor/comedian Fred Stoller, who appeared in a couple of Seinfeld episodes, took the tour with us, mostly to get a free ride to visit his mother. Adam took a picture of Fred and Kramer, which appeared in the book* Seinfeldia *by Jennifer Keishin Armstrong.*
>
> *Adam even got credit for the pic!*

Adam's Photo of Fred Stoller & Kenny Kramer

Here Comes the Boss...

Annie and I were in Palm Springs at the Ritz Carlton Hotel. We were waiting to be seated for breakfast when Bruce Springsteen walked into the restaurant with his son, Sam.

Annie and I couldn't believe our eyes.

Bruce headed our way. We introduced ourselves, shook hands, and of course, told him we were huge fans. After exchanging pleasantries, I looked for common ground.

"Years ago, when I was on the radio, I interviewed your mom and sister after you became famous." Bruce nodded politely.

"Can we take a few pictures?" I asked.

"Sure," said Bruce, who took my phone and passed it to his son, Sam. We got lots of pictures of the three of us, plus individual shots with Bruce. We took so many pictures that we were clearly monopolizing his time, but he didn't complain or blow us off.

"What brings you to Palm Springs?" I wondered.

Bruce joking replied, "a photoshoot."

Bruce Springsteen & Jeff

About a year earlier, the strangest thing happened involving Bruce.

I was sitting outside Morton's Steakhouse in The Woodlands, an upscale community outside of Houston. After enjoying a steak dinner, I was on the Morton's patio, smoking a cigar.

That's when five men around my age walked over and asked for a light for their cigars. I gave them my lighter. Then one of them said, "We're headed to the Bruce Springsteen concert at the Cynthia Woods Mitchell Pavilion down the street. We have an extra ticket—want to join us?"

My initial impulse was to say no, because the offer came so out of the blue, and besides—I didn't know these guys. But when they told me they had the extra ticket because their friend Jeff couldn't make it—I saw that as a sign. I'm big on signs.

I went with these fellows to the concert, and it turned out that one of my new acquaintances and I had mutual friends in the oil industry. Small world.

Bruce was great that night, as always.

Meeting Borat...

I love Sacha Baron Cohen.

Also known as Borat, Ali G, and Bruno, Baron Cohen is absolutely hilarious.

As many are discovering, Baron Cohen is also a talented dramatic actor. He played real-life Israeli undercover agent Eli Cohen in the Netflix series *The Spy*. In the early to mid-1960s, Eli Cohen spied for the Israelis while stationed in Syria. (Spoiler Alert!) Along the way, he befriended high-level Syrian government authorities and was privy to many state secrets. When his true identity was discovered, Eli Cohen was hung in a public square.

So, when I saw Sacha Baron Cohen enter the same Palm Springs restaurant the morning after Annie and I met Bruce, I was thrilled.

Sacha walked in with an older lady who he introduced to us as his mother-in-law. His wife, Isla Fisher, had already sat down with their kids.

Sacha and I had a brief conversation before he sat down. We talked about Canada and Seth Rogen. (I hadn't seen *The Spy* yet, or we would have talked about that.)

Sacha was a "landsman"—a Yiddish term for someone who comes from the same village or country—likely in Eastern Europe.

"Sacha, can we please take a picture with you?"

I knew he usually begged off taking pictures, especially because not everyone knows what he really looks like, minus his disguises and make-up.

As expected, he nicely said, "No pictures, please."

I said, "Even for a landsman?"

Sacha enthusiastically replied, "Especially for a landsman!!"

I Know You From Behind...

I have another stupid human trick. I have an actual ability to recognize famous people from behind.

As an adult, while standing in line to board a plane to Los Angeles, I could have sworn the man in front of me was Hal Holbrook, star of *Mark Twain Tonight!* I couldn't tell though, and he was carrying an awful lot of bags.

I was thinking, *Okay, would he be carrying all these bags if he were Hal Holbrook?* (Like he goes everywhere with his own porter or something...) Still, I was pretty sure it was him. I stuck my face out to the side so I could see the profile. Sure enough, it was!

So, I tap him on the shoulder. "Excuse me, Mr. Holbrook." He turns his neck around. "If you don't mind sir, I'd just like to shake your hand."

The man's got all these bags and suitcases in his hands. He's looking at me, then at the bags, and back at me again like, *Do you really want me to shake your hand, now?*

Very graciously, he unloads the bags from his right arm onto his left, puts the rest on the floor, sticks his hand out, and gives me a very nice, comfortable handshake.

Then, he bends down, picks up his bags, and resumes his place, looking forward in our line.

I had no idea if I was going to see or talk to him again, so I said,

"Mr. Holbrook, sir, if I may…"

He looked back at me.

"I just want to tell you that when I was a youngster, I had the privilege of sitting in the front row of your Mark Twain show in Montreal. You were looking right at me, and you made me feel so important with the expressive eye contact you gave me. It taught me something so important that I now try to share it with other people in my work as a communications coach."

By this time, I'm getting all sentimental and weepy-eyed. I'm talking to a man who has been instrumental in shaping my belief about the importance and power of our eyes.

As my emotions start to get the better of me, Holbrook says, "Oh, that's nice," and turns back to his place in line. A bit of a let-down for me, though I don't really know what I was expecting.

Once seated on the aircraft, I asked Holbrook, who was in the next row over, whether I could take a picture with him. He said no. That shut me down.

But once we deplaned and got into LAX, Holbrook came over to me and said, "Now, let's take that picture."

Redemption.

Hal Holbrook & Jeff

About my ability to recognize people from behind…

One day, I was leaving my office when I looked across the street and saw this fellow on the phone who had his back to me. The shape of his ears from behind gave him away.

I could tell it was Kiefer Sutherland, star of the TV shows *24* and *Designated Survivor.*

When he got off the phone, I walked up to Kiefer and found myself in full fan mode. "I love you man, I love you man," I told him repeatedly.

Kiefer was gracious—and posed with me for a picture.

Kiefer Sutherland & Jeff

Baby, I Love You...

Someone I always wanted to meet was Andy Kim, whose music I introduced in my demo tape years ago. Since that time, Andy went on to have dozens of hit records, including "Rock Me Gently." He also co-wrote "Sugar, Sugar" for The Archies. He did vocals for the song, too.

I love Andy's music. It symbolizes for me the '60s and '70s—when I met radio, my first love.

Andy's backstory is compelling. The son of Lebanese immigrants, he left his home in Montreal as a teenager and went to New York, taking only his talent.

I contacted Andy through his website. Though he had no idea who I was, I referenced the fact I was on-air at CKGM, a station that helped make him popular.

He never responded to my email.

But if you plant a seed…

A week or so later, I was driving along a midtown street, and there was Andy Kim on a walk. I pulled the car over and introduced myself. Andy politely claimed to remember my email and apologized for not responding.

We then got together for breakfast several times at the Four Seasons Hotel. When Spasi, the Four Seasons chef, would see Andy and me walking in, he would start to sing "Sugar, Sugar."

Andy had so many hit records, including "Be My Baby," "How'd We Ever Get This Way," "Baby I Love You," "Shoot'em Up, Baby!" "Rainbow Ride" and my personal favorite, "I Wish I Were."

With such a roster of music, over one of our breakfasts I suggested Andy consider a Broadway play of his life, documenting his songs, successes, and struggles. And this was before *Jersey Boys* came out!

Thinking of Spasi…

For a brief time, there was a show on TV about the richest man in New York. The part was played by actor Donald Sutherland.

In one episode, his butler asked what he would like for breakfast. "Poached salmon and Caesar salad," he instructed his butler.

Kind of a strange breakfast, I thought, but hey—it's a TV show.

A short time later, Spasi was preparing my breakfast when Donald Sutherland walked in and sat nearby. I chose not to disturb him, but I listened to him order breakfast.

"I'll have a poached salmon and Caesar salad," he told his server.

Spasi whipped it up in no time.

Is that an example of life imitating art?

Or art imitating life?

My Celebrity Shit List...

Random opportunity coupled with my media history opened the door to meeting many celebrities. Some were pleasant others, not so much.

I'll break many of the following stories down into two categories. The first category involves those on my Celebrity Shit List. (Suddenly, I'm thinking of Festivus and the airing of grievances.) The second category involves those on my Celebrity Hit List—people I admire and enjoyed meeting and talking to.

Number one on my Celebrity Shit List is Whoopi Goldberg. Whoopi tops it. The time I briefly met her was most unpleasant. She's someone that you couldn't pay me to now see in a movie or watch on TV.

I was having breakfast at the Four Seasons one morning with Andy, when Whoopi walked by our table. She sat down by herself next to us and ordered breakfast.

When Andy and I were done eating, I said we should head over to her table to say hello. Andy begged off, clearly uncomfortable with the notion. I should have trusted his judgment. Instead, I walked up to Whoopi. I'd seen many of her movies and enjoyed her acting.

"Ms. Goldberg, my name is Jeff Ansell. I'm a big fan."

I reached my hand out to shake hers, and she glared at me, not moving or saying a word.

I got the message really quickly. I walked away—a bit embarrassed.

Look, maybe her day was off to a bad start—I don't know—but she's an actress. The least she could have done was *act* friendly for the ten seconds our conversation would have taken.

No Hope for Bob Hope...

Bob Hope was another unlikeable piece of work.

Bob Hope was a Hollywood legend—a famous movie star and comedian. He appeared in many films, including a number of "Road" movies with Bing Crosby, *Road to Zanzibar, Road to Rio, Road to Singapore,* and so on. His movies were always good for a laugh, with Hope being the funny guy and Crosby, the straight man.

Hope was coming to Toronto to perform, and I succeeded in getting a phone interview with him prior to the event—only it didn't go as planned.

Hope and I were scheduled to do a phone interview about the upcoming show, but the only times he had available were on my two days off. But this was Bob Hope—surely it was worth me coming in on my weekend. My pleasure, in fact.

As instructed, I called Hope at the Miami Jockey Club, where I was told he would be. I was thrilled. I was actually about to speak with Bob Hope!

Or was I?

Hope kept me waiting for two hours before he could talk to me. Remember, I came in on my day off for this.

I was starting to get pissed at Hope. When he eventually got on the line and we began the interview, his answers were short and terse. Hope made me feel like I was intruding, bothering him, wasting his time. So, we were off to a stressful start, on my end anyway. I'm sure he didn't give a shit.

It got worse when I asked Hope to comment on the upcoming election between presidential incumbent Gerald Ford and Georgia governor Jimmy Carter. He got really pissed off at me. "I'm not here to talk about politics," snarled Hope. And with that—he hung up on me.

Later in the day, I received a phone call from Ward Grant, Hope's PR man, apologizing for his boss' behavior. Hope wanted to re-do the interview the next day—also my day off. Somewhat reluctantly, I said okay. Again, this is *the* Bob Hope we're talking about. It was worth another crack at it. Maybe this time, the tone of the conversation would be different—hopefully, friendlier.

So, the next day, we began the interview, all upbeat-like—when Hope suddenly started eating while he was talking. I could not make out what he was saying. His chewing was loud and disruptive.

Several times, I said, "Mr. Hope, it's difficult to understand what you're saying if you're eating. Would you kindly hold off for a few minutes until we finish our interview?"

Hope still kept eating. When it became clear I was getting nothing of value from this interview, I said, "Thank you, Mr. Hope, Goodbye," and hung up the phone. I ended it. Just like that.

Believe it or not, the PR guy Ward Grant actually called again, wanting me to take a third stab at interviewing his client.

Fool me once—shame on you. Fool me twice—shame on me. Fool me three times—I would need to have my head examined.

I already blew two days off. But I did ask a colleague if she wanted to do the Bob Hope interview.

She said yes, and guess what? Same thing happened. She hung up on him too.

Bob Hope—go figure.

My Celebrity Hit List...

At the top of my Celebrity Hit List—George Clooney. George Clooney is a mensch.

When Adam and I checked into our Los Angeles hotel, we noticed a lot of TV cameras and photographers hanging out in the lobby. They were waiting for George Clooney and Nicole Kidman to come down. Clooney and Kidman were upstairs in the hotel doing promotional interviews for their new movie, *The Peacemaker.*

Clooney had most recently starred in the movie *Batman and Robin,* and I wanted to meet him. So did Adam. So much so, that he and I sat in the hotel lobby for three hours, hoping to catch a glimpse and maybe get a fast hello with George Clooney when he came down from his interviews.

We hadn't even gone into our rooms or had lunch yet. Adam and I sat there in the lobby with our luggage between our legs, waiting for George. That's how concerned Adam was about missing "Batman" in person. Okay—I was too. After all, we had time invested in this—we needed a payoff on our investment.

In hour two of lobby-squatting, I slipped the concierge $20 to tip us off when George Clooney was coming down the elevator. The concierge discreetly palmed my double-dix and said he would let me know when.

Figuring we would be sitting there for possibly another hour or two, Adam ran to the downstairs candy store, where I later discovered he saw Nicole Kidman and got her autograph, vaulting her near the top of Adam's Celebrity Hit List.

Then, I got the big tip-off from the concierge.

George Clooney was in the elevator coming down, and Adam was nowhere to be seen!

Clooney walked off the elevator and out of the hotel's front entrance to briefly wait for his car. He was joined by his girlfriend of the time, Gisele Bündchen, who later married Tom Brady.

I approached Clooney, introduced myself, and we shook hands—but still no Adam.

Then, the valet pulled up with George's BMW. As he and Gisele slid into their seats, I kept a hawk-eye lookout for any sign of Adam.

Finally, in a moment of desperation, I said, "Mr. Clooney, would you please be kind enough to hang for a moment before you leave? My son Adam and I have been waiting literally hours to see you, and he's just inside, coming out."

"Okay, we can wait for a moment," George replied.

I nervously scanned the area. I didn't want Clooney to take off.

Still no sign of Adam.

"Mr. Clooney, thank you for your patience," I said, hoping I could squeeze another thirty seconds out of him.

When the half-minute passed, Clooney put his 7-Series into gear, so I quickly ran to the front of the car to block it from moving.

In my loudest voice, I yelled—"ADAMMM!!!"

That's when I saw the boy hurriedly run up to us. When Adam caught up to the car, he was out of breath.

"So, Adam, did you like my Batman movie?" George asked.

Though he was winded, star-struck, and unable to say a word, Adam did manage to vigorously nod—yes!

The next day, George was back in the hotel doing more interviews when we got on the elevator together.

George Clooney

I happened to mention that I'd read the cover story about him in that month's *Vanity Fair* magazine. The article mentioned that George originally wanted to be a journalist like his father, Nick. When I asked him about that, George self-deprecatingly said, "I wasn't smart enough to be a journalist."

What struck me in the elevator that morning was how gracious George was to everyone, even holding the door open for people.

Again, it's the little things...

Arnold, Kathy, and Desi...

Batman and Robin also starred Arnold Schwarzenegger as Mr. Freeze. Schwarzenegger was visiting Toronto to deliver a speech, and I purchased a VIP ticket for a photo with Arnold and a quick meet and greet.

Arnold Schwarzenegger & Jeff

Wanting to somehow connect with him beyond "hello, nice to meet you," I offered my condolences on the recent passing of his father-in-law, Sargent Shriver.

Arnold looked at me, paused for a moment, and said a heartfelt thank you.

Kathy Bates is also on my Celebrity Hit List.

Bates, star of *Misery*, *Titanic*, and two hundred other films, is one of the nicest celebs I've met—though it didn't start out that way.

Annie and I were downtown on Toronto's Yorkville Avenue when we saw Kathy Bates walking her dog. I called to her to say hello, and she briefly looked at me and continued on her way, which I thought was kind of rude. Annie and I continued on our way, walking in the opposite direction.

About thirty seconds later, I felt a tap on my shoulder and turned around. It was Kathy Bates. "Please, I apologize for not stopping a moment ago. My dog was in urgent need of relieving himself, so that's why I rushed by you."

Very nice of her.

One of the nicest celebrities I ever interviewed was Desi Arnaz, star of *I Love Lucy*, featuring his wife at the time, Lucille Ball. *I Love Lucy* was a top-rated TV show, one of the first to be shot before a live studio audience. Desi played Lucy's husband, Cuban bandleader Ricky Ricardo.

Arnaz had written the story of his life, including his relationship with Lucy, in a book entitled *A Book*. Our interview was conducted over the phone, and when we were done, Desi invited me to visit him at his home in Del Mar, near San Diego. I jumped at the offer.

When I arrived in California, I rented a car and started to drive to Del Mar. I called Desi to say I was on my way—and he begged off, telling me he was ill and not up to visitors.

Regrettably, Desi Arnaz died shortly thereafter.

Celebrity Space and Distance...

As bold as I was on occasion approaching celebrities, I also knew when to stay away and keep a distance.

Annie and I were in New York strolling through Central Park when we saw Yoko Ono walking toward us. Normally, I'd ask to shake her hand and maybe chat for a few seconds.

Then, I remembered it was a stranger who walked up to her and her husband John Lennon before killing him. The last thing I wanted was to trigger a nervous response by having another stranger walk up to her.

She may be famous—but she's still a person.

So, as we passed each other, I moved away to give her more space. I smiled at her, she smiled back, and we continued on our separate ways.

There are various measures of distance when it comes to proximity to other people. Anything more than fifteen feet apart is considered public space. Anything less than three feet is considered personal space. Intimate space is when you're literally in someone else's face.

So, when I saw actor Michael Douglas and wife Catherine Zeta-Jones in the lobby of the Four Seasons Hotel, I knew I had to say hello—up close, but not too close.

Certain they're regularly bombarded by people walking up to them, I headed towards them, stood three feet away—and asked their permission to step forward and say hello. I gave them the opportunity to say no.

They said yes, and during our brief conversation, we talked about Michael's dad, Kirk Douglas, one of my all-time favorite actors. Kirk Douglas was the son of Russian immigrants (born Issur Danielovitch) and was raised in Brooklyn. Later in life, Kirk Douglas rediscovered his Jewish roots and had a second bar mitzvah at the age of eighty-three.

"Everyone always asks about Kirk," Michael said with a laugh.

I was debating whether to tell Michael that, in the past, people would actually mistake me for him. I said nothing, though—I was concerned about insulting him.

Another time, Annie and I attended the premiere of *Life as a House* at the Toronto Film Festival. It's a highly engaging and successful film about a down-and-out divorced man who lives in a ramshackle house in one of the most beautiful areas of California.

For years, he's had a set of plans that he designed to create a dream home, but he never had the impetus to build it. Then, when he finds out he hasn't got long to live—he decides to tear down the old shack and build the home he's always imagined. The film was very moving. In fact, I wept like a baby.

In the theatre that night, sitting one section over in the same row was Kevin Kline, star of the movie. When the movie was over, the lights had gone up and the doors opened, we all walked towards the center aisle to head up the stairs to the exit.

It just so happened that when our two lines met, I was standing next to Kevin Kline. We stood waiting together to file out of the theatre.

It was another one of those moments. "Mr. Kline," I ventured respectfully, "I'm Jeff Ansell, and this is my wife, Annie. Beautiful movie. I thought you were fantastic."

"Well, thank you very much!" he said.

"You know, I'm sure you've heard this before—But you are this generation's Douglas Fairbanks," I said.

"That's very, very sweet of you to say."

Looking at him, I noticed his jacket was bunched up around the collar, and his tie was askew. Videographers, photographers, and fans were waiting at the top of the stairs—this was, after all, a world premiere. So, I said to him, "Mr. Kline, you look a bit disheveled. Do you mind if I straighten you out?"

"Please do," he responded immediately.

I adjusted his collar and straightened his jacket and tie.

"Thank you very much," he said—and then stepped into the sea of reporters and others waiting to take his picture.

He had been right there, standing next to me. How could I let it pass?

Another time, Annie and I were enjoying dinner at Due Ladroni (Two Thieves), a charming restaurant in Rome. We were on the patio enjoying our wine when an American couple sat right next to us.

The fellow did look familiar, but I couldn't immediately place him. Just then, the owner of Due Ladroni literally came running over to the American's table carrying a hardcover book and a Sharpie.

Knowing the fellow must be an author who'd reserved his table in advance, I glanced over to see the book. It was John Grisham's latest!

John Grisham, who has sold more than 300 million books, was having dinner at the next table!

After he signed the owner's book, I told Grisham I had been reading one of his books that day. He asked which one, and I told him—can't remember which now—then he chastised me for not reading one of his newer books.

Annie said he was joking, but to me—his voice had an edge to it. Grisham's wife Renee jumped in to friendly it up with us.

Still in Europe, Buzzie and I were in Paris at the Park Hyatt about to go touring, when exercise maven Richard Simmons walked toward us, wearing a T-shirt and his skimpy workout shorts.

There are two things I recall from that encounter.

First, the chain on my Chai necklace was tangled, and Simmons reached over to untangle it, which I thought was quite nice of him.

Then, I asked Buzzie to take a picture of Richard and me. After he took the shot, I told Buzzie he took a lousy picture, at which point Simmons chimed in, "Don't speak to Buzzie like that!"

Joining You on Your Flight...

I've had the opportunity to meet some pretty interesting people at airports and on flights, especially ones to Toronto, New York, and Los Angeles.

Headed to LA, the fellow sitting next to me looked so familiar—but I wasn't sure why. Had I seen him on TV? In the movies?

Turns out it was actor/comedian Eddie Griffin.[26]

When I brought out my laptop to work on my media book, Eddie asked what I was writing. I told him I was writing a book about how to communicate with the media. Like most other celebrities, Eddie had lots of beef with the news media. In our conversation, Eddie was giving me good quotes on his thoughts about reporters.

"Eddie, can I please record a short interview with you about media?"

"Alright, but I'm not a fan of media," he responded. Media outlets are "weapons of mass distraction," Eddie told me.

I used that quote in my book.

Then, there was the time I was at New York's LaGuardia Airport in the boarding area, about to get on a flight home to Toronto. Sitting next to me was a fellow wearing sunglasses indoors. But what really struck me was the length of this fellow's fingernails. They were really long. I mean extremely long.

He turned to me. "Are you going to Toronto for business?"

"No, I live there," I said. "I was just in New York for the day. What about you?"

"I'm a musician on my way to Toronto to do a show," he said. I wondered if I'd ever heard of him.

He stuck out his hand to shake mine. "I'm José Feliciano."

Holy cow! José Feliciano was famous for classics like "Light My Fire" and "Feliz Navidad," which he wrote.

What struck me most in our pre-board conversation was that José was traveling alone. Blind since birth, José was clearly independent.

When we stood up to board, I asked, "Would you like to take my arm as we board the aircraft?"

"Yes, thank you."

Once we got on the plane itself, it turned out we were seatmates. The conversation that followed was stimulating. José told me about his early years. We talked about his many appearances on *The Ed Sullivan Show*, one of the most popular TV programs of all time. We spoke as well about José's wife, who had recently become more dedicated to her Catholic faith.

At one point, José asked where the bathroom was on the plane. Again, I wasn't sure whether to get up to escort him. "Can I be of assistance, José?"

I waited outside the bathroom door until he came out so I could guide him back to our seats.

When we sat back down, José said, "I'm playing Casino Rama tomorrow night. Would you and your wife like to come?"

"I'd love to José—only it's our son's birthday and we have a family get-together planned."

"Bring everybody up as my guest," he said, "and I'll sing happy birthday to your son on stage." What a nice offer. I knew Adam wouldn't be into it though, so I politely begged off.

Before we disembarked, I knew that I couldn't let the moment pass without making a special request. "José, would you mind saying hello to my wife, Annie?"

"Not at all."

I dialed her up, but she wasn't home, so I left a message.

"Annie, you are not going to believe who I'm with now—José Feliciano! José, please leave a message for my wife, Annie."

José took the phone and left the following message:

"Hello Annie, this is José Feliciano. Are you happy, or are you married?"

Honest to goodness—Annie's saved the message to this day.[27]

On a return flight home from Los Angeles, I noticed the fellow in the next aisle was heavily tattooed. It was the tattoo on the left side of his neck that really stood out. Weird, I thought.

I went back to reading a paperback about a world-renowned soccer player married to a famous pop star. In the book, the soccer player turned out to be a wife killer.

Noting that the flight attendants were fussing over this heavily tattooed passenger, I wondered who he was. So, I walked to the front of the aircraft and looked at the manifest, which at that time was pinned to a cupboard in the plane's galley.

The man was David Beckham, the soccer superstar married to Victoria Adams, the former Spice Girl nicknamed "Posh."[28] A soccer player and a famous pop star—just like in the book I'd finished reading only moments ago.

Beckham and I stood next to each other as we disembarked the aircraft.

"I just finished a paperback—fictional—that is partly based on your life. Would you like to read it?"

"Yes, thank you," replied Beckham.

I handed it over with a warning: "Just so you know, they make your character a murderer."

Beckham seemed intrigued and took the paperback into his shoulder bag.

Another time, Annie and I were en route to Palm Springs via LAX. On the flight over, I went through the list of movies available to watch and chose a James Franco film. It's about a man accused of murdering his wife. In the middle of watching the movie, a fellow walked by me on the airplane, wearing a black baseball cap.

As he walked by, I realized—holy cow—"It's James Franco."

I chose a James Franco movie, and then he walks right by in the middle of me watching it. I debated whether to say anything to him—then decided I had to tell him what had just happened. So, I walked over to his seat.

He was taken by surprise when I told him that I'm in the middle of watching one of his movies. He seemed less than mildly enthused by my experience, but he shook my hand, and I returned to my seat.

The movie, by the way, was called *True Story*.

I first noticed this fellow after he told another passenger on our Atlanta-bound flight that he hoped she was having a wonderful day. Then, he complimented another passenger for her "lovely scarf."

He had a kind word for everyone boarding the aircraft. To me, sitting in the row next to his, he said, "That's a really nice suit you're wearing."

There was something magical about this guy. He had the ability to light people up and literally brighten their day. I knew he did mine.

He was so familiar-looking, too. After wondering where I had seen this tall, handsome, African American fellow, I suddenly recalled it was on the front page of the Wall Street Journal, *which had recently written about him.*

Keith Harrell is his name, and he is the author of bestsellers, including An Attitude of Gratitude.[29]

Keith is known for being a dynamic personal performance coach and a talented motivational and keynote speaker. Keith's way with people reinforced how easy it can be to touch other people's lives in simple, meaningful ways.

Jackie Mason Played it Straight...

My cousin Jeff and I met up in New York City for a weekend, in part to see Jackie Mason perform on Broadway.

Thinking I had an "in" because I've interviewed celebrities, Jeff said, "You're well connected. Can you get us in to meet Mason?"

I had no such "in."

At ten to eight Saturday evening, Jeff and I were heading into Jackie Mason's show, and there he was—Jackie Mason—standing on the street corner outside the theatre having a conversation with someone.

I nudged my cousin, and he nudged me back; we couldn't believe this. We politely hung in the background while Jackie Mason finished his conversation.

Mason looked at us over the other person's shoulder, as if to say,

"Hang on—I'll be there in a minute."

When he said goodbye to the other person, we walked up to him and introduced ourselves. "Mr. Mason, we're going to see your show tonight."

I guess we expected him to be funny with us because, after all, he's Jackie Mason. But he wasn't making jokes—he started to pepper us with questions!

"Are you going to any sights? What do you do for a living?" Jackie asked.

"I'm a veterinarian," Jeff said.

"Do you enjoy being a veterinarian?"

"I love it," my cousin answered.

Jackie then looked at his watch. "Listen, it's five to eight—I've got to get into make-up and get ready to go on. Let's finish the conversation after the show."

"After the show? Well, where should we go, Mr. Mason?"

"You see that door on the side?" said Mason. "Knock on the door and tell them that Jackie invited you after the show."

Thinking back, I wonder if Jackie being low-key with us was part of his pre-show ritual, one in which he focused on others or distracted himself prior to taking the stage in front of five hundred people.

We shook Jackie Mason's hand, just in case it was the last time we saw him. We were in a state of disbelief.

The show was great. When it was over, Jeff and I walked over to the side door—and knocked. "Mr. Mason invited us back to visit with him after the show."

"C'mon this way." The guy at the door took us into a small room upstairs, where three other people were also waiting to see Mason.

Ten minutes later, Jackie entered the room and sat down to chat with all of us as a group. Then, he went around the room and spoke to each of us personally. He asked about our wives, among other things.

Jackie Mason, Annie & Jeff

By showing interest in our lives, Jackie Mason made us feel important. That's a gift—maybe even as great as his comedy.

Every day, each of us has the ability to touch the lives of others in meaningful ways. To help people feel better about themselves.

CHAPTER THIRTEEN
Travels

Family vacations were always important to Annie and me.

When the kids were small, Annie and I took them to Marina del Rey. One morning, we went to a cafeteria-style restaurant, and standing in line nearby was a woman who had her back to me. Though I could only see her beautiful blonde hair from behind, I sensed it was Suzanne Somers. Sure enough, when she turned around, I was right.

She was there with her husband, Al Hamel, a producer and former TV host. It so happens that I had interviewed Suzanne over the phone many years ago as a radio journalist, when she starred in the hit TV show *Three's Company*.

So, I said to her, "Miss Somers, my name is Jeff Ansell. I interviewed you for a radio station in Toronto," (her husband, Al, is from Toronto).

"Oh yeah!" she says. "I remember."

Just at that moment, Annie walked up to the food counter to grab our breakfast trays, and I introduced them.

"Annie, I'd like you to meet Suzanne Somers and her husband, Al Hamel. Suzanne, Al—my wife, Annie."

Suzanne Somers will always have a special place in our hearts for two reasons. The first is she helped our family when we really needed it.

When Suzanne was a youngster, she had enuresis, described as involuntary urination, especially by children, at night. One of our family members experienced the same condition. Many so-called cures were available—most of them costly.

Then, we watched a video in which Suzanne discussed her problem as a child and said she was helped by a product put out by a company called Pacific Enuresis. The product was costly—hundreds and hundreds of dollars—which was a lot of money for us, especially then.

But the technology worked, Suzanne said on the video. She studied the product, talked with families and doctors, and stood by it.

On Suzanne's recommendation, and because we trusted her, we invested in Pacific Enuresis' technology. Within two weeks, the problem disappeared.

The product worked.

"I'm totally thrilled to hear that," said Suzanne.

After chatting for another brief moment, we went our separate ways to eat breakfast at picnic tables adjacent to the parking lot.

Reason number two for being so big on Suzanne Somers...

We finished eating at the same time as Suzanne and Al, and as we walked to our cars, I asked if the boys could please take a picture with her.

"Sure. Bring your kids over."

As I was about to take the picture of Suzanne with Josh and Adam, a car whizzed by in the parking lot. Instinctively, Suzanne stooped down and grabbed the boys so that they were safely kept away from the car.

And I thought to myself, Suzanne Somers, one of the big stars in Hollywood, is watching out for my boys right now. What a wonderful person to show such concern. Such a sweetheart!

Suzanne Somers and the boys

I also began taking holidays with each of my boys alone.

When Adam and Josh were twelve and eight years old respectively, I'd go away with each of them on separate weeklong holidays. Going alone gave us a real opportunity to focus on each other, connect even more deeply, and have fun at the same time.

The first time Josh and I went away together, we had no destination in mind. We packed a couple of bags and just took off. Josh and I had our baseball mitts in the car with us, in case we wanted to pull over somewhere to toss a ball around.

"Okay Josh, which direction should we head in?" Josh pointed east.

We drove for a couple of hours and then pulled over to play pitch and catch off the highway. That night, we ended up at the Ambassador Hotel in Kingston, Ontario. The hotel had an indoor water slide, and Josh loved it!

Josh and I also went to a Colorado dude ranch to ride horses. We stayed in a small cabin and had a blast living as cowboys. Another year, we traveled to Chicago—one of the highlights for Josh was dinner at Hooters. Later, on a trip to New York City, we took in all the sights and also got to see the Broadway play *The Producers*.

On our trips together, Adam and I went to the Denver Broncos training camp, Banff to play golf, Chicago for some deep-dish pizza, and the Northwest Territories to trout fish on Great Slave Lake. Adam caught a doozie!

On one of our trips to Denver, the parents of JonBenét Ramsey were holding a news conference on a local street corner.

JonBenét was the six-year-old beauty queen whose body was discovered by her father John in the basement of their home in Boulder, Colorado. At one point, John and his wife Patsy were themselves considered suspects in their daughter's murder.

Adam and I stood off to the side, watching the news conference unfold. It was live on CNN, so I called Annie to watch and see Adam and me standing behind the Ramseys.

When the news conference was over and the reporters dispersed, the Ramseys remained standing there on the street. That's when Patsy,

> *JonBenét's mother, looked at me, appearing as if she wanted to talk,*
> *though she had no idea who I was. Not wanting to bother her, I*
> *never approached.*
>
> *The family had been through enough without me poking my nose in.*
> *The crime is still unsolved and remains an open investigation with*
> *the Boulder Police Department.*

Busted in San Francisco...

For twenty-plus years, my brother-in-law Buzzie and I have taken summer trips together. Places we visited include Israel, Germany, France, UK, Denmark, and the United States.

On one of our trips, I got really stupid and careless. Buzzie and I were walking down the seamier side of Market Street in San Francisco when this Black fellow with yellow eyes approached.

"Want to buy some really good weed?"

This was before California legalized cannabis for recreational use.

"Sure, but I don't want a lot—just enough for a handful of joints because we're flying home in a week," I told him.

The fellow took me to an abandoned storefront a few feet away and gave me enough grass for about five days. We did our transaction on the street, though I did notice a homeless fellow clutching a bottle lying on the sidewalk nearby.

The marijuana was in tiny plastic baggies—big enough to roll one joint each. I shoved the bags into my pocket and walked away. Then, I got greedier. I turned around, walked back to the dealer. "Let me have one more baggie, please." He obliged. I paid him.

Again, we transacted discreetly—or so I thought.

Buzzie and I then continued our walk along Market Street. That's when we heard police cars with sirens blaring. We turned to look at the commotion caused by the cop cars. What's going on? Are the cops after someone? Are they on their way to a stakeout or hostage-taking? Has a bank been robbed?

None of the above.

The cops suddenly pulled up to Buzzie and me, jumped out of their cruisers, pushed me up against the wall, and handcuffed me. Standing amongst the cops was the "homeless" guy who was working undercover.

When they started to cuff Buzzie, I let them know he had nothing to do with my transaction and was not in possession of any marijuana. Buzzie wasn't a smoker.

The cops fished the little bags of dope out of my jean pockets. All this for six joints!

To say I was extremely worried is an understatement. I was concerned I would forever be barred from working in the United States. But more importantly, right now, I was worried about Buzzie. He was in his seventies at the time, and I feared for his well-being.

Then, the paddy wagon pulled up to transport me to the precinct. The cops gave Buzzie directions to the police precinct while they hauled me off.

Still handcuffed, I was hustled into one of three tiny cubicles in the paddy wagon. (By the way, the one I was in looked nothing like the ones you see in the movies and on TV.) The cubicles alongside mine had a small window separating us. I looked through the tiny window into the next cubicle, and there was the fellow who sold me the weed in the first place.

En route to the precinct, we went up and down big hills. After all, we were on the streets of San Francisco. My fear, among many, was if the paddy wagon tipped over, I would be trapped with my hands tethered to each other behind my back by the metal around my wrists.

Plus, I wasn't seat-belted in. If there were to be an accident, my head would literally have bounced off the walls and ceiling in my tiny cubicle space.

When we arrived at the police station, they put me into a holding cell. Considering I was such a badass criminal, San Francisco police officers handcuffed my handcuffs to a metal bar on the wall. That meant I was handcuffed to handcuffs, which were handcuffed to the wall.

I guess that was in case I was planning a getaway.

My cellmate was Leonard, the Market Street dealer. Leonard wasn't handcuffed at all. Why was I?

In our lockup, Leonard confronted me—an inch away from my face, in my intimate space as it were—repeating over and over, "Don't tell on me, man—don't tell on me, man."

After an hour in lockup, an officer walked into the holding cell. "Officer, I just want to know one thing. Is my brother-in-law here at the station?"

"Yes."

"How is he doing?" I asked, worried for Buzzie's well-being.

"I told him you're in the system," and with that, the cop turned and left. Buzzie later told me he freaked out when he heard I was "in the system."

At that moment, a siren went off inside the precinct. A riot had sparked in a nearby cellblock, so the entire police station was in lockdown.

When the lockdown ended two hours later, the arresting officer unbuckled my handcuffs (both sets), fingerprinted me, and filled out the paperwork.

I was scared—very scared.

When the officer told me to recount the events that brought me there, I kept calling him sir and it must have rubbed him the wrong way.

"Are you sassing me, boy?"

"No, sir—I'm just scared shitless."

The cop gave me a ticket, which ordered me to appear in a San Francisco court the following month. I was freed.

Once I was sprung from the joint, I was gratified to see Buzzie was okay. Naturally, he had been worried about me.

We then drove to Carmel, and once we settled into our hotel, I emptied my pockets on a dresser and discovered the police had inadvertently left a small baggie of you-know-what in my pocket. I made myself a nice fat one. For me, a pleasant way to end an unpleasant day.

But my problem was far from over. I still needed to make a court appearance in San Francisco in a matter of weeks.

I contacted my Toronto lawyer to help me find a San Francisco lawyer specializing in my need. That way, the San Francisco lawyer could appear in the California court on my behalf.

My lawyer located a fellow who would take on my case for a $5,000 deposit. Where was I going to get $5,000?

After all, Annie manages the finances in our family.

I wanted to tell Annie the truth as soon as I got home, but I was ashamed. Ashamed of being busted in California for buying a half-dozen joints, pointing once again to my teenager mentality. She may be right—perhaps I did peak at age seventeen with my first radio gig.

Annie could sense my anxiety and instinctively knew there was something important I was keeping from her. I had to tell her the truth.

When I did tell her, she was upset yet relieved to know my secret.

The day of my scheduled San Francisco court appearance, my US lawyer contacted me. "I don't know what happened or how it happened, but your case was never called."

An act of G-d?

CHAPTER FOURTEEN
Gratitude

Gratitude is so important in a person's life.

The Frank Capra Christmas classic *It's a Wonderful Life* is my all-time favorite movie. The film dates back to 1946.

Actor James Stewart plays George Bailey, an everyday fellow who owes big money to the evil town banker. Desperate as can be, George is about to commit suicide because, with his life insurance policy, he is worth more dead than alive. Exclaims George, "I wish I was never born."

That's when George's guardian angel, Clarence, comes to earth to grant him his wish—that he was never born.

Clarence then shows George how his not being born affected just about everyone in town. For example, when George was a child, he saved his brother Harry from falling through ice. Harry went on to become a war hero by saving the lives of two hundred soldiers. Because George was never born, every single one of those soldiers died as a result of George not being there to save Harry.

After witnessing several such examples of the impact his life had, George begs Clarence to be alive again.

It's a Wonderful Life made me realize how one person touches the lives of others without even realizing it. Frank Capra made several movies with similar heartfelt themes, including *Mr. Smith Goes to Washington* and *Mr. Deeds Goes to Town*.

I wanted to tell Frank Capra how his movies touched my life in a deep and meaningful way, but I didn't even know if he was still alive. So, when I was a radio reporter, I called the switchboard at Paramount

Studios in Hollywood and asked to speak to Frank Capra. I was asked whether I was looking for Frank Capra Senior or Frank Capra Junior. "Senior," I said.

To my absolute surprise, I was told that "Mr. Capra doesn't work out of this office. You can reach him at his home office near San Diego at 714..."

She gave me the number to Frank Capra's house!

I called him up. He answered the phone, his voice frail, with a slight stutter.

I said, "Mr. Capra? My name is Jeff Ansell. I'm from CFTR Radio in Toronto, Canada. I'm a reporter. Forgive me, are you the Frank Capra who made *It's a Wonderful Life?*"

"Yes, I am."

"I just wanted to say, sir, how much your movies have touched my life."

"That's very nice of you. Thank you, Jeff," he said.

Frank Capra was a wonderful man.

He once told the story of coming across on the boat from Sicily and how his parents were overwhelmed with tears when they arrived in America.

His movies always showed that no matter how desperate life may be, there's always hope.

His movies were about real people—decent folks just trying to do the best they can. Then, all of a sudden, life throws challenges at them, and these ordinary people have the chance to become extraordinary in their own way.

Frank Capra's films are beautiful, uplifting, and inspiring.

I told Mr. Capra that I hoped it didn't sound "corny" but that his movies, especially *It's a Wonderful Life*, impacted my life. Little did I know, at that time, Hollywood described Capra's movies as being full of "Capra-corn."

He chuckled in a nice, friendly way and very modestly said, "Thank you."

My Own Faith...

As a Jewish person, I wasn't raised with an overly strong sense of the philosophical or spiritual offerings of my faith.

My mother lit the Sabbath candles Friday nights, though we didn't observe most other traditions of our faith.

I did study for my bar mitzvah but found little meaning in it. Most non-religious Jewish youngsters learn to read Hebrew well enough to get to their bar or bat mitzvah, and then no more reading Hebrew or visits to a synagogue from that point on, aside from weddings, celebrations, and such.

> *There once was a synagogue that had a problem with mice. In order to get rid of the mice, it was suggested the mice be given bar mitzvahs. That way, they would never be seen inside the synagogue again.*

We did go to synagogue for high holidays like Yom Kippur (Day of Atonement). When I went to synagogue, the prayers were in Hebrew and I had no idea what was going on or being said. I kind of resented it. It was almost as if there was a secret handshake I wasn't privy to.

That was about to change. I was soon to learn more about my faith.

The morning my father passed, I slept in a hospital chair by his side all night. His breathing became quick and loud—a sign, the nurse told me, that the inevitable was close at hand. His life was seeping out.

It was 5 a.m., and I needed to call family members to tell them that now was the time to visit Dad.

You know what it's like when the phone rings at that hour of the morning. Your heart skips ten beats, and right away you expect to hear the worst.

In this case, we all knew what the worst was going to be, and that it was happening soon. But I didn't want to scare my mother and sisters more than they already were.

In my call to them, the first thing I said was, "Dad's resting now. He's sleeping." When they knew he was alive, they could calm themselves a bit and know that the worst hadn't happened—yet.

"You should get here real soon."

Following my father's death, I was emptying his dresser drawers and found the box with the macaroni lettering—the one that said, "Happy Father's Day—I like you, Dad."

He had kept the box all those years.

Mourner's Kaddish...

The day my father was buried, I said the Mourner's Kaddish for the first time.

The Mourner's Kaddish is a prayer said daily only by mourners, those who have lost a close family member within the last eleven months. The prayer is also recited on the Hebrew calendar anniversary of the loved one's passing.

The Mourner's Kaddish is a beautiful prayer that doesn't even mention the word death. Rather, the prayer celebrates life.[30]

So, it's ironic. Who are the ones chosen in synagogue services to reiterate the sanctity of life nearly seventeen hundred times a year? The mourners.

Ignorant about what was expected of me, I had no idea of how or when in the religious service to say the Mourner's Kaddish. Plus, my ability to read the prayer in Hebrew represented a challenge. I hadn't read Hebrew in more than twenty years. I was like one of the mice—only I came back.

Knowing I had no idea when to say the Mourner's Kaddish within the body of a prayer service, the rabbi asked his seven-year-old son to sit next to me to tell me when to stand up and say the prayer.

That was embarrassing—having to rely on a child to get me through Mourner's Kaddish. This child knew more about my faith than me.

Initially, reading the prayer phonetically helped me keep up with the other mourners reciting the prayer, who were more familiar with the ritual.

Part of the peace that the Kaddish brings a mourner is a reminder of the love they had for the parent they've lost. Each time the prayer is said in the presence of a quorum or minyan of ten Jewish men, the belief is we elevate the soul of the deceased, so they grow even closer to G-d.

When I said the prayer for my father and later my mother, I imagined their souls on their ongoing journey. And over the course of the unfolding year, I was able to find some peace with my father and my relationship with him.

Saying the Mourner's Kaddish is a huge commitment. Reciting it daily for eleven months in the presence of ten Jewish men represented a challenge, especially because of my travel. Throughout the whole time, for both my mom and my dad—I missed being in a minyan to say the prayer only a handful of times.

I remember being in Sault Ste. Marie, Ontario on business one day, trying to find ten Jewish men so I could say the Mourner's Kaddish for my father. Talk about needles in a haystack.

I did it, though. With the help of the local Jewish community, I rounded up the necessary nine men to say the prayer (I was the tenth).

On another occasion, Annie and I were in an airport on the way to Boston for a Harvard program, and I was upset to be missing a service at the synagogue.

Lo and behold, walking through the airport was a rabbi with a dozen of his students. We prayed together in a gate waiting area while I recited the Kaddish.

One time I missed being in a "formal" minyan was when I worked with the Grand Council of the Crees far into northern Quebec. Ain't no Jews up there, I can tell you.

I went to visit the Cree to share my knowledge of how best to use the news media to pressure the government and Hydro-Quebec into stopping the construction of an environmentally devastating dam.

The Cree owned ancestral land that the provincial power utility wanted to use for the creation of a giant hydro-electric project known as James Bay. The proposal for the dam involved getting rivers to flow backward, dislocating wildlife, contaminating sacred burial grounds, and displacing entire communities of people who had lived there for millennia.

My work with the Cree was part of the same campaign that

Robert F. Kennedy Jr. was involved with in the mid-nineties. I had the opportunity to meet Kennedy, a noted environmentalist, and we were pleased to help the Cree reach a deal with the government on James Bay development—a deal that greatly benefited the community.

> *Years ago, on holiday in Hyannis Port, Massachusetts, I was driving in front of the Kennedy Compound looking at their homes when a woman on a bike traveling at a good speed was headed straight for my car.*
>
> *I quickly veered away, as did the bike rider.*
>
> *I never told RFK Jr. that I almost killed his mother, Ethel.*

I was indeed the first Jewish person many of the Cree had ever met.

When I explained to my Cree hosts about the importance of the Kaddish prayer to me, they offered to join with me to make up a minyan. Though it may not have been the "proper" way to observe the prayer, the fact these folks cared enough to pray with me was wonderful.

We prayed together for my parents' souls to elevate—me in my way, they in theirs.

On my departure from the Cree community in Chicoutimi, Quebec, I was given a handcrafted wood carving of a canoe on skis as a gift of thanks. The Indigenous handicraft still has a prominent place in my den today.

Wood carving gift from the Cree

At the end of the eleven months following my dad's death, I actually led the congregation in reciting services in Hebrew—in an Orthodox synagogue, yet!

It was an overwhelming moment, like the climax to a movie. There I was, standing at the central pedestal upon which the Torah or holy scripture is placed and read. Fifty-plus men stood behind me, all of whom had grown up with the faith and were far more learned and comfortable in it.

As I led the service, I imagined that my father was standing beside me. I was very proud and hoped he would be too.

When my mother passed four years after my father, I again said the Mourner's Kaddish daily.

I recall the last Kaddish for my mother. I wept reciting the prayer for my mother that final time.

Part of the peace that the Kaddish brings a mourner is a thrice-daily reminder of the love they had for the parent they've lost. Saying the Mourner's Kaddish every day was my link to my mother, and before that, my father. I was afraid that with Kaddish being over, I wouldn't think about them every day when, in fact, I wanted to.

My first book, *When the Headline Is You,* is dedicated to my mother and father.

That was Annie's idea.

Minyan...

As my career unfolded, there were certain goals I set for myself. I wanted to be on radio, TV, write for newspapers and magazines, author a book on media and crisis communications, host a popular video series on LinkedIn, and appear in an award-winning movie—all of which I'm glad to say has been achieved.

There's at least one more big project on my bucket list. I want to create a limited TV series or movie that involves the recitation of the Mourner's Kaddish.

The idea is to take my experience hunting Nazi war criminals and marry it to a story about a son saying Kaddish for his father, a

Holocaust survivor whom he detests.

When I discussed the idea with Adam, he had so many creative ideas to tell the story that he did the heavy lifting in putting the screenplay together. Adam ended up taking over that project on my behalf. After all, Adam and I had attended several Robert McKee screenwriting courses in Los Angeles and New York, where Josh joined us. Turns out, Adam has a natural flair for compelling dialogue.

The story Adam wrote is so meaningful that reading it makes me laugh and cry—sometimes at the same moment.

Naturally, I gravitated to a four-step plan, this time, beginning with the result I desire.

Step #4 See Adam accepting the Oscar award for best screenplay

Step #3 Get the movie produced

Step #2 Connect with the right people

Step #1 Keep honing screenplay

We called the story *Minyan*.

Adam and I visualized Adam Sandler as the son saying Kaddish, Henry Winkler as his Holocaust-surviving father, and Jeff Bridges as the Nazi war criminal.

Adam submitted the screenplay to some of the world's largest screenplay contests and often made the quarter-finals.

Then—I met one of the world's greatest screenwriters who helped take the script to an even higher level.

When I took my seat on a flight to New York City, the man sitting next to me reached over, stuck his hand out, and introduced himself. "Hi, I'm Paul," he said.

I thought his introducing himself out of the blue was a bit unusual, but I stuck my hand out, shook his, and said, "Hi Paul, I'm Jeff."

Paul looked familiar. I knew I had seen him somewhere before.

He was holding his ticket in his hand, so when he turned away for a moment, I caught a glimpse of his full name.

Holy moly—it was Paul Haggis, the Academy Award-winning screenwriter of hits like *Million Dollar Baby* and *Crash*.

Paul Haggis & Jeff

And he's incredibly friendly! We started to talk.

When I introduced myself, Paul said, "I grew up in London, Ontario, and remember you from TV." That was neat. "I've been visiting my dad in London," he said.

"My son Josh graduated from the same school as you—Fanshawe College," I told him. "In fact, Josh heard you speak at the college one year."

I was dying to tell Paul about *Minyan*, the screenplay Adam wrote, but I didn't want to hit him over the head with it. He already told me that he was working on a new screenplay. I was afraid that if I started talking or asking about *Minyan*, he would shut down and ignore me for the rest of the trip.

I needed to find a way to casually introduce the subject into the conversation—at the right moment. The flight itself was a bit less than ninety minutes long, so at the forty-five-minute mark, I pulled the trigger.

"Paul, my son wrote a screenplay," I finally told him.

"Stop right there," he quickly responded. "I only make movies that I write."

"No, no—that's not why I'm bringing this up," I said, trying not to sound discouraged.

"There's a plot point in my son's screenplay that I cannot get my head around. Can I bounce it off you?"

"Sure," he answered.

There really wasn't a specific plot point I wanted to discuss—I just wanted to hear his thoughts on the story.

Now, in order for me to discuss the "plot point," I needed to take ten minutes to tell Paul the *Minyan* story for context. When I finished, he told me, Adam's story was "sweet" and "heartfelt."

"That's good to hear," I said. It was a nice validation of Adam's work.

Then, I asked about one particular plot point, and Paul went on to offer a critique of the whole story.

"Lose the flashbacks in the first act. Eliminate this character. Have this occur in the second act. Create this character for the third act."

Paul was offering so many insightful comments about the screenplay, and I wanted to capture each and every one. I figured if I brought my phone out and recorded him talking, he might turn off. So, I took notes, but the only paper I had nearby was a napkin.

Feverishly, I jotted down Paul's ideas. I soon ran out of napkin space and started writing on the air sickness bag—both sides. When I ran out of space on the vomit bag, I grabbed the airline magazine and started ripping pages out.

I told Paul that, for me, meeting him was an act of G-d. He said thank you, adding he did not believe in G-d. (For context, Paul was earlier embroiled in a Church of Scientology controversy.)

As we were disembarking, I wanted to ask if there was a way for us to stay in touch, but I thought it might be too pushy. So, it surprised me when Paul offered me his coordinates in case I ever needed to talk with him again. What a wonderful man.

I typed up all my notes for Adam, put the scraps of paper and the air sickness bag into a baggie, and gave it to him. After inputting Paul's ideas, Adam's contest performance elevated *Minyan* from quarter-finalist to semi-finalist.

I told Adam, "When you accept awards for best screenplay, be sure to hold up this baggie and thank Paul Haggis."

What Are the Odds?...

Adam Sandler was in town filming the movie *Pixels*. The shoot was near my downtown office.

As I was leaving my office on a Thursday afternoon, I thought to myself that I would print a copy of *Minyan* just in case I ran into Adam Sandler, as unlikely as that was to happen.

I printed the screenplay, threw it in my knapsack, and headed to the hotel next door where I parked my car every day. As I waited for the elevator in the hotel, who do you think walks up to me?

Yep. Turns out, Adam Sandler was staying in the hotel. You can see in the photo how freaked out I was to bump into him.

"Mr. Sandler, my name is Jeff Ansell."

Sandler, very friendly, said, "Nice to meet you."

"My son Adam has written a screenplay specifically for you. I have it in my knapsack. May I please share it with you?"

"There's a better way to do this," Sandler said. "Here's a number for someone to contact at my Los Angeles office and tell them I told you to call."

I did call—nothing ever came of it.

But hey, you've got to buy a lottery ticket to win. When I heard that Henry Winkler was coming to town for a fundraiser—I knew Adam and I had to be there. Henry Winkler was also on our wish list for Adam's screenplay *Minyan*. He was perfect to play the main character's (Adam Sandler's) father.

Adam Sandler & Jeff

After purchasing two VIP tickets to the Winkler event (just to make sure we met him), Adam and I had a private moment with the former Fonzie.

He had four hundred people waiting for him to speak, and when Adam and I pitched him—he politely begged off from further conversation, saying, "I'm overwhelmed."

Well—we tried.

Henry Winkler & Jeff

Then, there's Jeff Bridges. He made me cry.

One year, during the Toronto International Film Festival, Adam and I were in the lobby of the Hazelton Hotel when we spotted Jeff Bridges standing there.

I've had my kick at the can many times when it comes to approaching celebrities. It was Adam's turn now to make contact. He would be the one to walk up to Jeff Bridges to pitch his screenplay.

Adam was nervous, and so was I. My concern was that Bridges would tell my son to take a hike.

So, I said to Adam, "If he tells you to screw off, say 'thank you, Mr. Bridges' and walk away."

Mustering up courage, Adam walked up to Bridges.

I didn't want to stare, so I used my peripheral vision to watch the encounter unfold. All the while thinking to myself, please be nice to my boy.

Adam walked up and said: "Mr. Bridges, my name is Adam Ansell, and I've written a screenplay with you as a lead."

I held my breath, wondering what would happen next.

That's when Bridges put his arm around Adam and said: "Come on Adam, let's take a walk," and they did.

Tears came to my eyes. Jeff Bridges was being kind to my son, making him feel like a million dollars.

Two minutes later, they returned to the lobby, with Adam clutching a piece of paper that had the name and number of Bridges' agent on it. Nothing came of it, but like I say, you don't get if you don't ask.

If, as a result of reading this, someone wants to produce the TV series or turn it into a movie—go for it. Though *Minyan* at the moment remains a work in progress, encountering Paul Haggis, Adam Sandler, Henry Winkler, and Jeff Bridges—was not just a sign.

To me, it was a giant billboard, I hope, of what is yet to come.

Faith...

I've met many famous people over the years, but the most courageous person I've ever met is Kim Phúc.

Few know her by name. Most know Kim as the nine-year-old child seen in the iconic Pulitzer Prize-winning photograph taken during the Vietnam War in 1972.[31]

Just Google "Vietnam War photo," and this image comes up. The photo is of Kim running naked on a road after being severely burned on her back by a South Vietnamese napalm attack. Kim was initially in the hospital for fourteen months and has had a score of surgical procedures, including skin transplantation.

Kim and I were speakers at a convention in Scottsdale, Arizona. She was the speaker immediately before me. Kim had everybody in the conference hall, including me, in tears as she recounted her painful ordeal.

Kim Phúc & Jeff

I respectfully say that she was one tough act to follow, which I had to do. Talk about switching gears!

Due to constant pain, Kim had considered suicide. Then, in 1982, she found a New Testament in a library. The book led her to become a Christian.

In *Christianity Today* magazine, Kim wrote: "I had so much hatred in my heart—so much bitterness. I wanted to let go of all my pain. I wanted to pursue life instead of holding fast to fantasies of death … I invited Jesus into my heart. When I woke up that Christmas morning, I experienced the kind of healing that can only come from God. I was finally at peace."[32]

Kim's profound faith enabled her to forgive.

It's with pleasure that I can report Kim is doing well and living in Canada.[33]

CHAPTER FIFTEEN

What Was in My Heart

After talking about all these stories, the experiences I've had, and people I've met, I debated whether to include this story in the book. However, I want *Who I Am After All* to be an honest representation of my life so far—so I'm going to tell it.

This story has nothing to with celebrities or investigations or anything like what you've read up to now. This story is about how my mother died and the guilt I felt in her death. It cuts to my core.

I was devoted to my mother.

In 1995, she suffered a mild heart attack. With the family in agreement, her doctors determined she would need a triple heart bypass operation, a relatively routine procedure—or so I thought.

We unquestioningly listened to the doctors who told us, "Your mother is going to be fine. The operation will add years to her life."

The day of her surgery, Mom told me and my sisters, "I'm scared I'll never see you again."

Coming from her, the words were jarring. Almost as if she knew.

Instead of responding directly to her fear of imminent death, I remember trying to be dismissive of her worry. "Mom, it's a common operation. You'll be fine in no time. Plus, we'll see you in a few hours. It's going to be okay—you'll see."

I thought by not acknowledging her fear, I would help her feel more positive. I was wrong. My mom began to cry. I had never seen such fear in her.

"Mom, you'll be up and around tomorrow," we said, parroting what the doctor told us. Moments later, orderlies wheeled her into the operating room.

It was the last time we saw my mother alive.

Her first operation ended at 6 p.m. The triple bypass heart surgery was declared a success. While she was in the recovery room, my siblings and I joined a couple of other close relatives for dinner in a nearby restaurant.

Arriving back at the hospital later, we were shocked when told our mother was now in critical condition. The triple bypass didn't take.

"We've got to bring her back into surgery and try again," the doctors told us.

At 1 a.m., the doctor came into the waiting room.

"The second bypass didn't take either. We're going in a third time."

At 4 a.m., in the dead of night, the doctor came into the waiting room.

"I'm sorry, but there's nothing we can do," he told us.

"What do you mean, there's nothing you can do?" I said, starting to get worked up.

The doctor began to back away from me, and I realized what he had meant. "Where's my mother now?"

"She's on life support. What would you like us to do?" he asked.

"Bring our mother back to us."

They went to get her.

At that moment, I collapsed to the ground. My legs just gave way, and I fell to my knees.

I had collapsed too when my father died four years earlier. I've since seen others fall to the floor when confronted with terrible news like this.

The nurses and orderlies wheeled my mother into the Intensive Care Unit. She was hooked up to various tubes, heart monitors, respirators, and IVs.

My sisters and I wanted to be with her one last time. To give us privacy in the middle of this big room, the nurses pulled a curtain around us.

They couldn't see us—but they could hear every word we said.

We needed to say goodbye to our mother.

Nothing had prepared me for this moment.

Knowing she could hear us through her coma, I said the Shema, the same prayer she taught me when I was a child. We told her how wonderful a mother she was, how dearly we loved her, and how she would live forever in our hearts.

Standing there silently, we knew we had to do what had to be done. It was a terrible moment.

Outside the curtain were the nurses.

I will always remember the one nurse who came in to unplug my mother's life support machines. The nurse was weeping. I was so touched that a stranger was moved as deeply as she was by my mother's passing, a woman she never knew.

In the weeks and months that followed, my personal guilt intensified. Why hadn't I done more research beforehand, to learn about the risks of heart bypass surgery?

I made a living asking important questions—yet I had failed to ask enough, or the right ones, before my mother's death. Questions like— if a bypass doesn't take the first time, can you re-open my mother and try again? Are you able to try a third time? Is there a risk our mother could die?

It turned out that during the first operation, her doctors had actually operated on two people simultaneously, my mother and another heart patient.

I asked the doctor later, "Would my mother still be alive today if you were operating only on her?"

"Well, maybe..." was all he said, sheepishly.

But that was now hindsight. My mother was dead, and I did nothing to prevent it.

I was plagued by my mother's death.

Saying Kaddish for my mother three times a day for almost a year kept us linked. Kaddish was my daily reminder of her.

My Turn...

Days after the Kaddish for my mother was over, I began to feel considerable discomfort in my chest. It was a burning sensation—almost like a bowling ball on fire in the center of my chest.

I was sure it wasn't my heart. After all, the heart is on the left side of the chest and shaped like a Valentine, right? Being a man, I never told anyone, including Annie, about the pain near my heart.

Plus, I was busy. That week I was off to San Francisco to work with PG&E, then do a Toronto session the morning after, and following that, I needed to go home and pack. We were moving homes in less than a week, and I had set aside three days when I got home to pack my clothes, belongings, and many tchotchkes I had collected over the years.

I never got to do that.

When I was in San Francisco, the pain in my chest came back—worse than before.

A glass of water always helped me extinguish the fire in my chest, as would resting for five minutes or so afterward, just to catch my breath.

I was coaching eighteen people that day in California, and thankfully, I got through the session without incident. When I finished the training session at 5 p.m., I hung out at the airport until my 11 p.m. red-eye flight home.

Landing in Toronto at 7 a.m., I went straight to my downtown office, took off the clothes I slept in, put on fresh clothes, and conducted a full-day training session. I did this after having chest pains hours before taking the overnight flight home—only to go straight to work.

For the first time now, as I sit here writing this, I see something was seriously wrong with that picture.

In those days, Annie worked with me. I finally told her about the pain.

She made an after-work appointment for me to see our family doctor. He, in turn, insisted I see a cardiologist first thing the next morning. Their office made arrangements for the immediate appointment.

Before I left the house the next morning for the doc's, Annie asked, "When are you coming back?"

"I'll be home in a couple of hours," I said, confident in my ability to keep my promise.

Picking up my car keys, I kissed Annie goodbye, opened the door, and left for the hospital. To this day, I still have not been back in that house.

After my initial examination and stress test, I put my shirt and socks back on.

"Where are you going?" asked the cardiologist.

"I've got a meeting to go to, and then I need to go home and pack. We're moving next week."

"I don't want you to go anywhere," said the heart doctor firmly. "The test results are clear—something is very wrong with your heart."

I was not expecting to hear this.

"I want to check you into the hospital now and do further tests, so I know for sure what we're dealing with."

"Yes, but I've got to go," I insisted.

"Listen to me carefully," he said. "Your life is on the line here. You have severe blockages in three of your arteries. One of your arteries is 100% blocked—the other two are 75% and 50% blocked, respectively."

Those were big numbers.

"In my opinion, unless you have emergency triple heart bypass surgery, there is a 2% chance you'll be alive in a year."

My mother had died a year earlier during heart bypass surgery.

I had come full circle. To me, the need for possible bypass heart surgery was a message from G-d, or my mother, or maybe both.

The message was that since I felt such guilt for my mother's death—I would go through the exact same operation as her. It was as if G-d was telling me, "You feel responsible for your mother's death? You weren't—but if it will end your guilt, I'll give you the same operation as her. Then, you can stop blaming yourself."

"How long am I going to be in the hospital?" I asked the cardiologist.

"I can't tell you," he said. "It depends on a number of factors, including your personal recovery time."

I had just started a new business, Jeff Ansell & Associates, and this was yet another setback.

I called Annie to come to meet me at the hospital, along with the cardiologist, Dr. Marty Strauss. When Annie met him for the first time, Marty broke the news to her very gently. Annie began to cry.

Marty will always have a very special place in our hearts. When he saw how upset she was, Marty started to cry too. He has since become a dear friend.

Had I been shlepping boxes as part of our move, it might have been too much for my heart. I might not have survived the year. Annie later said some people would do anything to get out of packing—even subject themselves to heart surgery.

That weekend, while I was in the hospital, our friends came to the rescue and helped pack our entire house.

By now, you know that I believe in signs. On the day of surgery, Annie told me she kept seeing women in the hospital who looked like my mother.

Despite being shocked and scared throughout this ordeal, Annie remained strong. She was my anchor—upbeat, caring, and supportive in every way.

The following Tuesday, Annie, Adam, and Josh moved into our new house—without me. To this day, we still have some unpacked boxes in storage, and none of us knows what's in them.

I had other concerns as well. One year earlier, I had quit my full-time job at Hill and Knowlton, the PR company. Working on my own now, I was running a business with no backup. I had just bought a new house, and now I was about to cancel three months of paid consulting work because of heart bypass surgery.

All this was very hard for me to do.

While waiting for surgery, I called clients to say, "You know that meeting we have next week? I'm going to have to postpone it for seven weeks or so."

When they asked why, I said I have a personal matter to tend to. I didn't want clients to think I was checking out. I still wanted their business afterward. But telling them the whole story just didn't seem right. Despite this book, I'm not used to sharing the details of my life. And I certainly wasn't then.

Depending on my relationship with the client, I would sometimes say it's "a minor health issue." If I knew the client well, I'd open up and tell them the truth. I was confident I could count on them to understand and be there to help me in the future.

To add insult to injury, some of my clients then asked, "So who can you suggest doing the work?" and I needed to refer them to other coaches and trainers.

I wasn't only losing their business; I was now giving it away to my competition!

But I've always believed G-d made enough for all of us.

Then, I had the triple bypass.

A Glass of Water...

I remember waking up from surgery. Opening my eyes, I could see I was in the recovery room of an intensive care ward. There were other beds around and lots of doctors and nurses flitting about.

A tube had been stuck down my nose and throat to help me breathe. Unable to move and having no desire to, I didn't feel much of anything—except being parched.

I desperately wanted a drink of water. Because of the tube, I couldn't have anything in my mouth.

Days later, upon discharge from hospital, I was taken to my new home—a place I had been inside only once, when I bought the house. I was immediately ushered into the master bedroom. I wasn't even sure where the bathrooms were.

My first night home, I was having a horrible time sleeping. I had become used to sleeping on a hospital bed after the operation, one that tilts up if you're having problems while lying flat.

Triple bypass heart surgery puts the body through severe shock. First, there's been the trauma of the operation. After cutting into the chest, the breastbone and ribs are broken, the heart and the lungs are stopped, and a number of other internal organs are slowed. After the operation, all these organs need time to return to normal function.

One also loses a lot of muscle strength lying in bed for nine days and faces the constant pain that comes with almost any kind of movement. I felt like an old man—weak and fragile.

Some people talk about depression as being a side effect of having a major surgery or illness. That didn't hit me right away.

But what happened—and I wasn't expecting this—is that I lost all my confidence.

Up to then, I had a fire in my belly. That's what gave me my edge. I was afraid I would never get it back.

I was heavily dependent on Annie, my boys, and my friends for meeting my almost every need.

And I lived in fear of sneezes. Every time I sneezed, it was like time stood still as I wondered whether my chest would blow open and my guts would spill out.

Some time that first night home, I woke up gasping for breath. I thought I was going to die. I was experiencing night terrors.

Annie got very frightened, and the boys came running into our room. Adam, thirteen, and Joshua, nine, were scared. It took me about ten minutes or so before I could breathe regularly and calm myself down.

That Friday, Annie made the first Sabbath dinner for us in our new home. Up to this point, I mostly stayed in bed with brief exercise walks from room to room. Stairs, however, were a challenge and difficult to maneuver. Putting on a bathrobe, I made my way (with help) downstairs, one step at a time.

It was the first time I'd seen the main floor of my new house since coming home. Annie led me into the kitchen and to the table. I didn't even know which seat was mine because I hadn't sat there before! Slowly, I sat down at what became the head of the table. The boys were beside me. Annie lit the Sabbath candles. I said the Friday night Sabbath prayers, looked at my wife Annie, and sons Adam and Josh, and I began to cry.

Emotions filled me, and I couldn't stop weeping. I felt grateful to be alive, to be with my wife and sons, and to be able to sit at that table.

They were tears of gratitude. Why gratitude? Quite simply because I was allowed to live. I could breathe. I got to see my family again.

These things loom large when you're on the edge of losing them, as my mother had, and I almost did.

Waking up in that hospital recovery room with those tubes down my throat, I was thirstier than I'd ever been in my life.

To this day, I still think about that experience, and most every time I drink a glass of water, I say a special prayer. That's how appreciative I am for something as simple as water.

I even thought of calling this book *A Glass of Water.*

CHAPTER SIXTEEN
After All

Regrettably, the tears of gratitude turned into tears of sadness a number of years later when I was diagnosed with cancer. When I thought about including my cancer in this book, I wondered what I could possibly say on this terrible subject that hasn't been said before.

Turns out, a couple of things.

Up to then, I had done everything possible not to even use the word "cancer" in my vocabulary. I was superstitious about illness. So much so that I wouldn't even walk or drive over a handicapped parking spot.

I found out I was ill while I was literally packing for my annual summer trip with Buzzie—this time, to Alaska. That's when my family doctor called with a sense of urgency in his voice:

"Your blood test results from two days ago came back," he said. "They're waiting to see you now at Women's College Hospital to talk about the results."

It couldn't be good.

The signs were there—night sweats, fever, weight loss.

When I got to the hospital, they immediately put me through a battery of tests and scans. I was floored by their diagnosis and in a daze, quite literally, for months.

Cancer only happened to other people. Not to me.

Having been diagnosed and, over time, given a treatment plan, I just wanted to get through the ordeal, which seemed to worsen daily.

I was experiencing pain, growing loss of memory, deep depression, high anxiety, poor eyesight, weak hearing, constant stomach upset, nausea, zero appetite, no taste buds, extreme fatigue, and growing loss of memory (did I already mention that?)

My memory gaps are now so wide I could plan my own surprise party. Speaking with others and remembering what they say has become a challenge. The chemo impacted my memory center, so thoughts evaporate quicker than a blanket on fire. I often need to say, "Remind me what we're talking about."

Needing a Recovery Plan...

I didn't think about it then, but beyond getting by day to day, I had no real plan and no actual vision for what was ahead—beyond misery.

Focusing on steps to get better—physically and emotionally—wasn't exactly at the top of my mind because pain, depression, and anxiety got in the way.

I needed a roadmap to see me through this ongoing nightmare. I needed a plan, or else I would fall into the trap of wallowing in my own despair. The stakes were too high.

My life literally now depended on the four steps I chose to guide me through the worst time of my life.

First things first—determine the treatment program.

Step #1 Follow doctors' orders

I took the meds they wanted me to take, the unpleasant chemotherapy sessions they told me to endure, and underwent the arduous bone marrow transplant they said had a 50 percent chance of success.

I trusted my docs and made a point of staying away from the internet for info about my ailment. In fact, since being diagnosed, I've refused to Google what any of my symptoms might have represented.

The health care professionals who treated me were great. They used a team-based approach in my treatment, and more often than not, the left hand truly knew what the right hand was doing.

Of course, the one or two who didn't, stand out. Some health care people would speak to me as they would a piece of meat.

One time, I lost it and got testy with a nurse in the hospital who I felt was very terse with me just before I was about to have eye surgery. She was lacking any degree of apparent warmth and was just firing off questions, without any regard for whether she was talking to a human being or not.

What really bummed me out was when she asked me which eye they were operating on. She asked as if she had no idea.

I know that question is probably asked before all such surgeries. I had the impression, however, that she was clued out. I said out loud I didn't want her near me.

Then, of course, I felt terrible after because I lashed out at her, failing to realize and recognize that she might have had a difficult day. You never know what's going on in someone else's life. I tried to apologize as profusely as I could because I felt so bad about my uncalled-for outburst.

With all the needles, injections, IV drips, and such, I felt like a pincushion. I don't like needles. I don't think anyone *likes* needles. So, every time I received one, I had a rehearsed schpiel for the nurse or health care worker.

"Please use the short needle, please be gentle, please warn me before you put the needle in, and please talk to me about something else while you're putting the needle in." Annie heard me say it so many times she would mouth the words to my monologue.

Doctors also told me I couldn't work anymore. My illness forced me to close my downtown offices and training studios, which I had operated for close to twenty-five years. I had to let my staff and colleagues go—including my close friend Richard Maxwell, also known as Rob Richards (his real name).

Rob and I had been on the radio together and were colleagues in training thousands of people. We've been close friends for forty-five years. Before we met, I heard him on the radio in my car. I thought he was super talented, so I called him out of the blue. I told him who I was and that he was so good he should be working at CHUM, and soon after, he was. We've been tight ever since.

Rob Richards & Jeff

I felt bad closing up the office—a source of livelihood for Rob and, of course, me. But cancer and the treatment involved gave me no choice. When business came my way after I got cancer, I would send it to Rob for him to work on.

Besides, I was so unmotivated to work—I didn't open my laptop for fourteen months. I couldn't even motivate myself to be motivated. I had hundreds of emails piled up—some important, I suppose. But I didn't care.

I told one client why I couldn't work with her, and she started to cry over the phone. Though she and I hadn't known each other long, we connected on a deeply meaningful level. Her genuine empathy warmed my heart.

Step # 2 Experience cancer with dignity

I wanted to the best of my ability to maintain dignity throughout my ordeal. That didn't last long.

My first of more than a dozen chemotherapy sessions was punishing. During the six hours my initial chemo treatment lasted, I went into spasms and wasn't responding verbally due to a bad reaction to one of the chemo drugs.

When the treatment was done that day, Annie and her close friend Elaine brought me home, literally carrying me into the house.

For months, I was weak. Walking a few steps left me exhausted, short of breath. My only real daily exercise was walking up and down the fourteen stairs in our home at least three times a day. That by itself often knocked me out. I also had never noticed the steep incline outside our front door before. At least, it never seemed steep before.

When I would wake up in the middle of the night at home, I would pass the mirror and see my reflection. That was my overnight reminder that I had cancer, just in case I had forgotten during my sleep.

Before I knew it—I wasn't even making it to the bathroom on time, pissing myself. Humiliating.

My dexterity has been compromised as well.

Cancer and its treatments often cause loss of agility in fingers. My fingers are numb, as are my toes, making it challenging to not only type but also to walk, even around the block.

Chemotherapy screws with your appetite, and it took the foods I love to keep me eating. My weight was down to 127 pounds. The problem was, most foods I loved were deep-fried or generally bad for me.

So, when I had a chance to eat my favorite deli food, I jumped at it. I had soup and a sandwich. Immediately after starting to eat, I realized the challenge ahead. I couldn't hold the soup spoon because my hand was shaking—again, the result of chemo. The pastrami sandwich I ordered quickly slipped through my fingers and fell apart on my plate and on my lap.

Just tying my shoelaces and buttoning my shirt can take fifteen minutes each. Once, I got so frustrated trying to button my shirt, I ripped the damn thing off and the buttons went flying. Annie buttoned my shirt this morning.

Princess Margaret, the local cancer hospital, placed me in isolation for a three-week period prior to a bone marrow transplant. No family. No visitors.

I had already had fourteen chemotherapy treatments, many of

which were highly toxic, some of which required extensive hospital stays.

This upcoming twenty-one-day treatment was the longest I would be away from Annie in our forty years of marriage.

On my way to the cancer hospital for the long stay, I found myself saying out loud, "I don't want to go." Then, I started to sob uncontrollably—afraid I wouldn't be coming home.

All I could think was that I wanted one more time.

One more time to hug my grandkids.

One more time for a family vacation.

One more time...

On some days during my hospital stay, I got ready for bed at 2 p.m. Sleep was difficult because each hour I had to piss like Secretariat due to the nonstop IV saline drip and the boatloads of water they made me drink.

I got the Sunnybrook suite, the corner room on one of the sides. I would spend just about all day looking at one branch straight out my window standing up pointing skyward. That's what I'd do with the day, just look at the branch.

The view from my room at Sunnybrook

With my IV pole not able to reach the bathroom, I needed to urinate into a jar. The jar would fill up quickly. Twice, in the middle of the night, I dropped my jar and its contents splattered all over my bed and me.

One of the times I dropped the jug was after I hiccupped violently, and the jar fell to the floor, spilling everywhere—trapping me on my bed.

Another time, the nurse was changing the urinal jug, and the bottom of it opened up and spilled all over me. At this point, if I were an investigative reporter, I would have put the manufacturer out of business.

The bone marrow transplant itself was grueling for a variety of reasons, including one that required the use of adult diapers.

My ship of dignity sailed without me.

By the way, the surgical procedure on my eye required me to be awake, though I was earlier told I would be knocked out with a general anesthesia. So, when I didn't get one—I freaked out at the idea of people touching my open eyeball.

I will admit to being very squeamish—especially when it comes to my eyes and my tuchus.

As they started the procedure, I heard the doc say things like "clamp the eyelid" and so on. I had visions of *A Clockwork Orange*, the movie. That also freaked me out—so I figured I needed to anesthetize myself.

The way I did it is by yapping incessantly. Talking nonstop doesn't give me time to think about what they're doing to me. So, I told the doctors and nurses in the room stories—as they were operating.

Stories about Nazi war criminals, closing up a nursing home, and exposing bad doctors (not a good choice really, given the audience). I even threw in the *Seinfeld* story.

That was for my left eye.

If I ever have the procedure repeated in my right eye—I will need new material or a whole new operating team.

Truth is—I didn't want to be awake during any of my hospital stay. After the nasty effects of my bone marrow transplant kicked in, I just wanted to sleep each day away.

To be able to endure this, I would be forced to redefine my

interpretation of dignity.

People—friends and family alike—ask for details on the type of cancer I was experiencing. Despite my openness in this book, I am private about some matters, including details like those.

"Don't ask me about my specific illness, my treatment, or my test results," I told people. "You can just ask how I'm doing and if I want to say more, I will."

If I share more than I want to, I know they'll be online like a bullet to see my chances of survival. If the odds are good according to their expert of choice, they will faithfully report the good news to me. If the news isn't so good according to other sources—not so much.

As I mentioned, I was sometimes mistaken for Michael Douglas in my younger years with my dark and wavy hair. Personally, I never saw it. With my hair loss and diminished eyesight, I now look more like Alan Arkin, and that's on a good day.

By the way, believe it or not—if you're a man, having your hair fall out has a bit of a benefit. There's no need for regular haircuts or daily shaves. Today, I am as bald as a cucumber and have no idea whether my expensive hair transplants will bear fruit once again. Hey, it's cancer—no guarantees.

Besides, I've got much bigger fish to fry.

After I got sick, what I did *not* want to hear from people was, "Oh, you look so good" (subtext—". . . for someone battling cancer").

To me, statements like that invite trouble. People no doubt mean well when they say, "you look good," but I don't want to hear it. I don't need any canaries.

No Pep Talks Please…

The last thing I want to hear from people, family and friends alike, is motivational speeches. They often piss me off more. Unless the pep talk is from someone who has themselves experienced cancer or lives with someone who has cancer, they generally have no clue.

It's easy to tell somebody to "eat"—only the smell of food can be revolting, and sometimes enough to induce gagging or worse.

Six months or so after my initial diagnosis, docs told me the treatments had worked.

Was it a canary? The docs just gave me good news. Could it possibly have been a canary?

Though I was still feeling the impact of the massive doses of toxic chemo I'd received, I felt well and recovered enough to drive to a restaurant to meet Jeffrey Leeson for breakfast. Jeffrey, the co-author of my media book, was visiting Toronto from his home in Minnesota, and our breakfast was purely social.

After we finished eating, the last thing I remember about that breakfast was putting my coat on—because I fainted. Right there in the middle of Eggspectation.

"Your legs just crumbled," Jeffrey later told me.

The next thing I vaguely remember is being put into an ambulance with paramedics and Jeff. They rushed me to the hospital for more poking and prodding.

Annie joined me soon after I arrived. Turns out, my cancer was not only re-emerging—it was also spreading.

They took my driver's license away that day. I still don't have it back.

Step # 3 Avoid destructive narratives

There have been many mornings where I wake up crying.

At the height of my cancer battle, I wanted to commit suicide. I just wanted to die. I was sick of being sick.

When the side effects of my cancer and its treatment kicked in bigtime in the first few weeks and months after my diagnosis, I plunged into a deep depression.

At the height of my depression, I certainly wasn't feeling gratitude. Anything but.

In fact, I was resentful.

I don't quite remember saying this, but my cousin Jeff reminded me of it the other day. He said that after one of my treatments, I told him I resented healthy people. More than that—I was jealous of healthy people.

I did briefly feel that way, and I'm ashamed of it, embarrassed even, to say those words. I made myself into a victim and now feel guilty about that.

I truly wish this on no one.

I certainly wouldn't say that now because no one knows what goes on in the lives of others. In some ways, everybody has some load to carry.

But I was angry. Pissed that I got cancer.

In the beginning of my illness, I was plagued by the question of why. Why did I get cancer? Why me? What did I ever do to deserve cancer?

I suppose everyone with cancer thinks about that in the beginning.

I always thought that if I were a relatively decent person, then good deeds would protect me. Over time, I stopped asking myself why I got cancer. I think I know the answer. The answer is *because*. It's that simple.

I wasn't scared of dying. I was more frightened of being forgotten. That once I crossed over, people, including family and friends, would never think or speak of me again. That thought frightened me.

I've got such mishigas (craziness) in my head that I can't even listen to songs like "Don't You (Forget About Me)"[34] by Simple Minds and Glass Tiger's "Don't Forget Me When I'm Gone."[35]

Out of sight—out of mind. That's a fear.

I even thought about the music I want to be played at my funeral. Two songs in particular, and they've got to be played in order.

The first song is "Turn! Turn! Turn!"[36] by The Byrds, which speaks to the impermanence of life.

The second song is "O-o-h Child"[37] by The Five Stairsteps. "O-o-h Child" is about healing after a loss.

Alex Trebek of *Jeopardy!* passed away recently. I heard him say in a pre-recorded interview that a week or two earlier, he himself wanted to die. Not so unusual for cancer patients, I guess.

Few people, except those who have experienced cancer and its treatments, understood what I was going through.

The funny thing is when I mentioned my suicidal thoughts to most people, including my oncology psychiatrist—no one flinched.

That told me I wasn't the first cancer patient to say that out loud. I was afraid that when my psychiatrist, who specializes in cancer patients, heard me threaten suicide, he would get the straight jacket police after me.

> *I gave Annie permission to kill me. Smothering me with a pillow would be fine. I told her I would record a video and get a lawyer's letter authorizing her to do me in.*
>
> *That way she'll be off the hook.*

Negative thoughts had a powerful grip on me during much of my treatment. Once I would get the negative thought, I'd then tell myself a story feeding the thought, and thereby create a narrative that led to a dead end.

It didn't always take much. Sometimes it was a word somebody would use, or a tone in their voice could trigger my predictable reaction.

Language is important—what we tell ourselves and what others tell us. Words matter.

During one of my chemo treatments, a young doctor came into my hospital room and said, "I want to discuss your 'aggressive' cancer and possible need for 'palliative' care."

I never heard any of my doctors use the word "aggressive" before in describing my cancer. That scared the crap out of me. Plus, to me, the word palliative means near death.

I told the doctor to leave and not return. Words are powerful. Doctors ought to know better.

When he left my room, all I could think was that I was dying. I had an aggressive cancer and might need "near death" care.

During my hospital stay, there were three of us in a room with two nurses on duty. A nurse that was not assigned to me walked by, and I asked, "Nurse, can I trouble you for a moment?" Her blunt response was, "No, I'm not your nurse." She should have said, "Even though I'm not your nurse, let me go track down yours." It's the same message with a completely different effect of kindness.

The tone of voice of others also influenced my self-serving

narrative. Some people would speak to me in a sorrowful tone—like I was on the threshold of crossing over.

Other times, people, mostly family and friends, would put on a happy voice thinking that would cheer me up. It didn't. Normal voices are fine.

Home all day, every day—what to do with myself? Most days, my most important decision has been which baseball cap and T-shirt to wear.

I would read and watch TV until my eyes hurt. There has been many a day when I would just sit in my den, lights out, just think-ing—mostly about cancer and my fate. That, of course, led to a hor-rific narrative unfolding in my head in which I wasn't going to make it—one of the motivators for this memoir.

I broke one of my key rules this morning. I did something stupid. I went on the internet.

For the past few days, I've had an itch in an upper part of my body. I went online to look it up, and I read that an itch in this specific part of the body is a symptom of the cancer I had experienced. That would have meant my cancer was spreading.

Right away, I went into a funk, having visions of more punishing chemo. I was awfulizing, thinking the worst.

I debated whether to tell Annie. But I didn't want to keep anything from her, so I told her. Her hands immediately went to cover her mouth.

I know what she was thinking—"Please G-d, not again!"

As tempting as it was to explore a dark path in that instant, I called my doctor instead. I confessed to him that I went online, told him what I saw, and thanks to camera phones he quickly diagnosed the cause.

I know too that, despite my occasional bouts of depression, I need to bite the bullet and know that this too shall pass.

Many a time, I envisioned myself as already being healed.

Step # 4 Savor the journey

If anyone deserves to talk about the power of appreciating life, it's my friend Lynda Fishman.

When Lynda was thirteen years old, she lost her mother and two younger sisters in an Air Canada crash, which killed everyone on board.

The life that followed was harsh for Lynda. Her father never recovered from the shock of losing his wife and two daughters. He withdrew, leaving Lynda alone in the world at an age and time when she needed loving and parenting the most.

As Lynda says, "Not a day has gone by where I haven't thought about my family who I lost almost forty years ago."

Yet, she had the strength and courage to struggle her way through and is today a sought-after speaker on the subject of gratitude. Lynda's book *Repairing Rainbows* is the story of how she and her husband Barry built happy, fulfilling lives for themselves.[38]

To confront my depression, I would think about Lynda and all that she's been through.

In particular, I was mindful of a blog Lynda kindly wrote about me several years ago. Whenever I'm down on myself, I re-read what Lynda wrote and it reminds me of the person I strive to be—someone who's not only grateful but also eager to show appreciation to others.

Below is Lynda's blog post, from June 11th, 2010:[39]

> *Whether someone is just doing their job, volunteering, or exceeding expectations, gratitude goes such a long way. Genuine, intangible, heartfelt gratitude and appreciation. It is the most powerful form of recognition that anyone can provide. And it's incredibly wonderful to be on the receiving end. The positive energy, aka positive vibes, are so strong it is sometimes possible to see the physical effects. It ignites others. And most of all, it feels great for everyone involved.*
>
> *This morning I had the privilege of spending time with a very good friend, Jeff Ansell, who does communication and media training. Jeff knows that every time I talk about the tragic death of my mother and sisters, I have trouble controlling my tears. In order to prepare me for my upcoming book launch, Jeff offered to pull out the big guns and provide me with some anti-crying strategies. No guarantees of course, but at least the tears will be less immobilizing.*
>
> *I picked Jeff up at 6 a.m. so we could drive downtown together and beat the traffic. The first thing he did when he saw me was to thank*

me so much for picking him up. (He is helping and training me, and he's thanking me. I would have picked him up in North Bay!) But that sweet and sincere "thank you" set the tone immediately. And then I watched as Jeff spread his magic throughout the early morning hours. We stopped for breakfast and he thanked the parking attendant, he thanked the host at the restaurant, he thanked the waiter, he thanked the chef. He doled out continuous, genuine, intangible, heartfelt gratitude and appreciation by saying thank you (really saying thank you) and smiling at each and every one of them. He did it so naturally and so sincerely, I don't even think he realized the effect he was having on these people. But I did. They smiled back. They obviously felt his gratitude for them and for what they did, despite the fact that they were just doing their job.

He appreciated them. They appreciated him. It was like watching a gift exchange. . .

When someone says thank you and really means it, their gratitude makes its way right into your heart. I think we are incredibly lucky to understand and appreciate the value of gratitude in life.

It continues to amaze me that there are people like Jeff who thank others profusely for the smallest things, and sadly, there are others who will take and take without ever feeling grateful.

Ungratefulness breeds greed and jealousy.

Gratitude breeds abundance.

Thank you, Lynda.

Those words have carried me through some despondent times, especially during moments when my mind is clouded with deep despair and I can only think about myself.

Just so you know, in my coaching session with Lynda that morning, I was in tears before her.

At the time, I felt a need to re-connect with people, like my nephew Jonathan Goldstein. I shared my regret that we were never close when he was growing up and that I felt absent from his life.

Jon, who is Dina and Buzzie's son, is well known in his own right.

As a writer, Jon authored, among other books, *Lenny Bruce is Dead, I'll Seize the Day Tomorrow*, and *Shmelvis: In Search of Elvis Presley's Jewish Roots* (he also produced the documentary film of the same name). Jon appeared for years on NPR's *This American Life* with Ira Glass and served as host of CBC's *WireTap*.

Then, when he went to work for Gimlet Media to host the podcast *Heavyweight*, Jon did a special on Buzzie's troubled relationship with his older brother Sheldon. It's well worth listening to.[40]

The fact that Jon lived in Brooklyn while I was in Montreal didn't help us be closer. When Jon moved to Montreal years later, I was already living in Toronto.

After I expressed what I felt was our lack of memories together, Jon wrote me:

> *Hey Jeff,*
>
> *Getting the sense of how you'd felt in some ways absent from my life inspired me to send along some memories, to assure you that, in my mind, you were very present, loomed large.*
>
> *Here are some:*
>
> *My first memory of you is from Brooklyn. You were standing on our long red velvet couch, looking into the small wall mirror as you fixed the fallen eyebrow from my Ernie and Bert puppet under your nose. You wanted to see what you'd look like with a mustache.*
>
> *I remember when you first moved in with Annie. I remember you both making chili when Michael Jackson's "Rock with You" came on the radio and how you both started dancing together.*
>
> *I remember your trip to Montreal when you were on crutches after burning your foot making French fries.*
>
> *I remember at probably five years old when you took me in your orange Datsun to see Ronald McDonald. I remember how you shifted me around your lap trying all kinds of different positions to make me comfortable.*
>
> *I remember hearing about your fight at McDonald's with some*

anti-Semite, how you grew so furious you blacked out. That's what real resolve looks like, I thought.

I remember the gifts you gave me for my bar mitzvah. The ring with the J just like yours.

I remember turning to you in Schneiders restaurant when I was a teenager and asking you why our family was the way it was, and you said maybe it was something in the breast milk.

I remember photos of your awards that Pop Moe and Grandma Bookie kept under the glass on their dresser.

I remember when you carried me into the kitchen looking as though you were holding me by a fistful of hair but really had me by the seat of my pants.

I remember how at your wedding you began your speech by thanking your parents for having you and how brilliant and funny I thought that was.

I remember spending the day with you at CITY as you chased a story. It was a busy day, but you insisted on stopping for lunch with me and the cameraman. I think we had Italian.

I remember us riding with Josh to an Expo game and that you got angry at the honking cars in traffic who might wake him as he napped in the back.

I remember once being so depressed we talked on the phone and you really cared, tried so hard to yank me out of it. I remember you saying, "it really is a wonderful life."

Beautiful words. Thank you, Jon.

Live...

What keeps me out of the abyss now and serves as motivation? Mindfulness helps. Paying attention to my thoughts rather than falling victim to them.

Above all—I need to remember to keep breathing.

Having cancer, more than a dozen chemo treatments, and a bone marrow transplant can be pretty overwhelming. In those anxious moments, it helps to recalibrate through breathing, especially when negative thoughts creep in and create an upsetting narrative.

Though I still teeter on the abyss once in a while, I'm driven by the need to always have something to look forward to. It doesn't have to be fancy. Buzzie taught me that.

When he was in the US Army, for example, Buzzie always looked forward to the next meal. Army food, no less.

I've just discovered there's a small radio station in my community that broadcasts in English and other languages. Maybe when I'm ready, and if they're willing, they'll let me work there a couple of hours a week. Back to where I started, which is kind of cool.

Most of all, looking ahead, I'm driven by my desire to dance with Annie at our grandchildren's weddings.

The burden on Annie has been tremendous.

I'm so grateful she's my wife and is navigating this difficult journey with me. Annie brought me back to life. She did everything for me. I am blessed she said yes to marrying me. I truly do not know how I would function in this world without her love and without her by my side—rarely complaining about the attention I need.

And if she does complain about me—most always, it's because I deserve it.

Everything I went through—Annie went through too.

Annie and I have a vision. We see each other being very old, holding hands in the kitchen. I love that girl so much.

Annie

In the moments where slivers and slices of gratitude sneak through the clouds, I discover it has been the prospect of dying that has been teaching me about living. About appreciating the blue skies and even the grey ones.

About truly living in the now, as tempting as it is to fret over yesterday or worry about tomorrow. These are goals worth striving for.

You've likely heard the saying, "Yesterday is history, tomorrow is a mystery, today is a gift. Why do you think they call it the present?"

These days, I sit outside a fair bit. I look at the trees, watch people walk by, meditate now and again, and am just happy to *be*.

There have actually been moments where, rare as they may be, I've looked upon my cancer as a gift. My cancer reminded me I was alive. My cancer reminded me of the fragility of life.

Writing this book has been important to me. Mostly, it has provided me with something to do during the day besides watch *Blue Bloods*. It has given me added incentive to jump out of bed in the morning, eat breakfast, and then start writing all day.

More importantly, writing this book has let me retrace the random pathway of my life, allowing me to genuinely connect with memories—some pleasant, others, not so much.

Telling my stories—even to myself—has given me added insight into why I am who I am. I'm motivated by what the re telling of these stories has done for me.

I want to live now.

Just like George Bailey says at the end of the movie *It's a Wonderful Life*, "I want to live now. Please let me live."

Putting together *Who I Am After All* has been an important part of my recovery—therapeutic in a way, I suppose.

My journey thus far has been a magical, incredible ride—even with the cancer and even with the childhood I had.

I now feel fortunate to have grown up as I did, blessed with the life that followed.

My name is Jeffrey Ansel.

ADDITIONAL PHOTOS

Family Picture

ANSEL. To Mr. and Mrs. Moe Ansel (nee Beatrice Latofsky) on December 31st, 1955, at the Jewish General Hospital, a most welcome son, brother to Diana Barbara and Eileen Brenda. Both doing well.

Jeff's Birth Notice

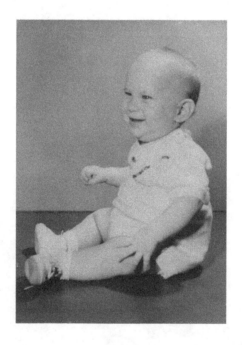

Baby Jeff

Baby Jeff and his sisters

Jeff in high school

JEFF ANSELL
"It's better to remain silent and
thought a fool, than to speak up
and remove all doubt" (advice to
F. M.). PROTO: James Tayler.
FAV. EXP.: Solid gold rock and
roll. AMB.: Disc-jockey. PROB.
DEST.: Taxi-dispatcher. ACT.:
Pres. of the Apathy Club, but
who cares? CH. MEM.: My
"CHALUSHADIKA" Jeans.

Jeff's high school yearbook

Disco Jeff

Annie & Jeff on their wedding day

Young Jeff

Richard Maxwell & Jeff representing CHUM at a Marathon

Jeff's CHUM Photo

Jeff's TV debut

Governor General Edward Schreyer, Brian Thomas, Annie & Jeff
at the Governor General Award Dinner

Invitation to the Governor General Award

Dave Powers (special assistant to President John F. Kennedy) & Jeff

Jeff on TV

Jeff in the Newsroom

Jeff in the Newsroom

Jeff talking to Sydney Poitier

Richard Simmons & Jeff

Annie & Jeff

Kenny Kramer, Adam & Jeff

Fred Stoller, Adam & Jeff

Annie, Rae Appleby, Elie Wiesel & Jeff

Rob Stewart & Jeff

Gord Martineau (news anchor at CityTV) & Jeff

Jeff in his 40s

Ed McMahon & Jeff

Maury Chaykin & Jeff

Paul Burrell (Princess Diana's Butler) & Jeff

Margaret and Wallace McCain & Jeff

Jeff at ABC News New York

Clinton Dinner Ticket

President Bill Clinton & Jeff

President Bill Clinton, Annie & Jeff

Jeff Communications Training Publicity Shoot

Jeff Communications Training Publicity Shoot

Jeff Conducting Communications Training Program

Isaiah Thomas & Jeff

Adam, Josh & Jeff

Granddaughter Mia & Jeff

Grandson Jake & Jeff

Mia & Jake

Buzzie & Jeff

Bruce Springsteen, Annie & Jeff

Justin Trudeau & Jeff

Jeff giving a speech at CADA (Canadian Automobile Dealers Association) conference

Jeff's Communicating with Confidence profile picture

Jeff giving a speech at IACP (International Association of Chiefs of Police) conference

Former CIA Director General David Petraeus & Jeff

When the Headline is You book

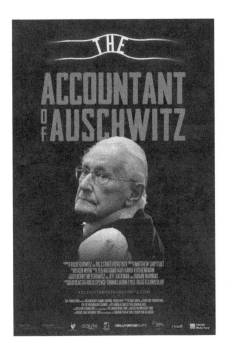

The Accountant of Auschwitz Movie Poster

Korean copy of When the Headline is You book

AFTERWORD

By Adam Ansell

I wanted nothing to do with this book.

Initially, when *Who I Am After All* was an untitled Word document, it was easy for me to hate.

And I hated it.

I thought it was morbid.

I wanted to see that energy directed at the future, not the past.

Every time Jeff showed me a passage he wrote, the font would go up in size. The cancer spread to Jeff's eyes, so the bigger the font, the worse his health. The document became a measuring stick. By the end it was at size 613.

Still, it never crossed my mind that Jeff wouldn't make it. Call it a delicate blend of optimism and denial.

So, from my perspective, watching a 65-year-old guy with 25 years left in the tank waxing retrospective didn't sit well. There were bigger fish to fry. Jeff had another lifetime left to live.

Jeff always wanted to write a book about his life. He took a stab at one the first time he almost died in the mid-90s. Emergency triple-bypass heart surgery is as good a motivator as any to get it all down on the page. Both the book and the death didn't take. It never crossed my mind that he wouldn't make it then, too.

When Jeff wanted to brainstorm topics for this book, I gave him passive aggressive eye rolls. When Jeff pitched me story ideas for this book, I gave him one-word answers. In turn, I'm not acknowledged in the acknowledgements.

Jeff isn't pitching stories or pecking away at his keyboard one index finger at a time anymore. The book is here. Jeff isn't.

This time, both the book and the death took.

After avoiding this book for over a year, I picked it up. Reliving some of the stories I'm featured in with fresh eyes, I saw some of Jeff's best qualities – compassion, confidence, and chutzpah – in a new light.

I'd forgotten Jeff used his body as a human barricade to block George Clooney's BMW from leaving the Century Plaza Hotel for an unreasonable amount of time. All so Clooney could ask 13-year-old me if I liked *Batman* and I could nod yes like an idiot, too nervous to say, "Actually, I'm more of a *From Dusk Till Dawn* kind of guy".

When we ran into Clooney the following day at the elevator he asked us, "Didn't we do this yesterday, guys?" Yeah, but we're just heading up to our room. Call it a coincidence. When we all stepped into the elevator, Jeff brought up Clooney's father doing the news in Cincinnati and just like that they were chatting like old friends.

"If Jeff Bridges tells you to screw off, say thank you and walk away." I never thought much about why my father kept saying that. He had no idea how Jeff Bridges might react to me. Now I see he couldn't help but worry about how I felt. It never occurred to me his concern was for my feelings on the chance the encounter didn't go as planned. I was 25 at the time, not immune to rejection, but old enough to take it. Especially on a long shot like that.

We had fun together. It wasn't supposed to end.

Then Jeff's prognosis went from all clear and in remission to being given weeks left to live, and what was supposed to be didn't matter.

Jeff stopped sleeping after that. Afraid he'd never wake up. Tomorrows were in short supply, and he wouldn't risk any of them.

So, on no sleep, no food, and no health, fueled on weed, vodka orange juice and an unbreakable will to cement his legacy to the page, Jeff put the finishing touches on his second autobiography and his second death.

The funeral home sent two ladies to collect Jeff's remains. One, a grizzled vet. The other, a wet-behind-the-ears rookie. The rookie made a rookie mistake and nearly dropped Jeff's lifeless body.

While my mother and brother stood frozen in their mortification, my eyes raced to find Jeff's. I could always make Jeff laugh at the weird and inappropriate with my eyes. It took a couple of seconds for the realization to set in that our eyes would not meet. Now or ever.

Every day since, something sparks that realization.

Jeff completed the book on fumes. At the very end, his hearing, sight, and strength were gone. On book calls, Jeff's once booming, unmistakable voice was extinguished, reduced to a labored whisper. I saw how much this meant to him. How it put him at peace.

Jeff may not have had 25 years, but he had enough left in the tank to finish his book.

A book for the real McCoy is a shit trade-off. But, if that's as good as it's gonna get – and it doesn't ever get that good for most people – I can live with it.

Jeff isn't here anymore. But *Who I Am After All* is, and it always will be.

ACKNOWLEDGEMENTS

With appreciation to friends, colleagues, and reviewers, including Sharon Appleby, Jordan Berman, Jeffrey Chernoff, Inge Christensen, Pat Folliott, Hersh Forman, Tracy Holotuk, Jon Hussman, Judith John, Renée Kaminski, Elaine and Sid Kohn, Jeffrey Leeson, Stuart Lewis, Howard Lichtman, Victor Malarek, Janice Mandel, Richard Maxwell, Jack Muskat, Matthew Shoychet, Steve Skidd, Roy Thomas, Greta Wakelin, and the FriesenPress Team.

Thank you to my Harvard colleagues—Larry Susskind, Michael Wheeler, Andrew Wasynczuk, Brian Hall, and John Beshears.

Eric Hellman—thank you for documenting many of the stories. Tim Laing—thanks for partnering on *Pillers of Parkdale*.

To my physicians—Dr. Matthew Cheung, Dr. Graeme Schwindt, and Dr. Marty Strauss—thank you for saving my life.

With gratitude to my mentors including Casimir Stanczykowski, Robert Holiday, and Earl Jive.

Jonathan Goldstein, thank you for your guidance along the path.

NOTES

Chapter One: Who I Am

1 *Mark Twain Tonight!* was a one-man play performed by Hal Holbrook from 1954-2006. A clip of his performance is on the New Jersey Performing Arts Center's YouTube channel here: https://www.youtube.com/watch?v=H0WAuqdrqL8

Chapter Two: Wanting

2 Listen to Earl Jive on the radio in 1974 in this YouTube clip: https://www.youtube.com/watch?v=dtxHZtGCplI&t=179s

3 The original YouTube interview is on my YouTube channel at the following link. I start talking about my outfit at 00:48. https://youtu.be/VvWzMs177RE?t=48

Chapter Three: I Lied My Way onto the Radio

4 A news piece about Lee Marshall and his work as Tony the Tiger is in this clip from ABC: https://www.youtube.com/watch?v=pRzGV1x74ds

5 Mickey Rooney is among the old-time movie stars dancing in a compilation video on YouTube set to Uptown Funk. Although the whole video is a must-see, Rooney has a couple of brief seconds in it at the 00:26 mark (wearing a cowboy hat) and at 2:27 (wearing an old-fashioned tuxedo.) The video is here: https://www.youtube.com/watch?v=M1F0lBnsnkE

6 A clip of me visiting the Canadian National Exhibition in August of 1983 is here: https://www.youtube.com/watch?v=L_xqD8ke2F8

Chapter Four: Confronting Jew-Haters and Hunting Nazi

7 I recommend reading Ernst Zündel's Wikipedia page to learn about his Holocaust denial stance and the harm he caused: https://en.wikipedia.org/wiki/Ernst_Z%C3%BCndel

8 An article in the *Toronto Sun* quoted that line from a review of Zündel's book, published in the neo-Nazi *Liberty Bell* magazine here: https://torontosun.com/2017/08/07/ernst-zundel-deserved-agony-not-a-quiet-exit

9   A clip of my reporting on Zündel's court appearances on the *Who I am After All* YouTube channel: https://youtu.be/UYuY9m78f6U

10 More of my reporting on Zündel is in this clip on the *Who I am After All* YouTube channel: https://youtu.be/czgzv23dTHY

11 Here's the article Mark Bonokoski wrote for the *Toronto Sun* in 2017 after Zündel died: https://torontosun.com/2017/08/07/ernst-zundel-deserved-agony-not-a-quiet-exit

12 My reporting on the topic of Nazi war criminals in Canada is in the following clip on the *Who I am After All* YouTube channel: https://youtu.be/r0TCdptV5rk

13 The photo of Helmut Rauca is from a CBC documentary, *The Helmut Rauca Case,* which can be viewed here: https://www.cbc.ca/archives/entry/the-helmut-rauca-case. There is another documentary about Rauca on the History Channel's YouTube channel here: https://www.youtube.com/watch?v=hIjcZaUfndo

14 Faigie's original article can be found on my website here: https://www.jeffansell.com/newsfeed/2018/2/1/faigie-schmidt-libmans-story

15 My article about Haralds Puntulis can be read in its entirety on my website: https://www.jeffansell.com/jeffs-war-criminals-article

16 The link I sent Howard Blum with me discussing the Nazi investigation is here: http://www.youtube.com/watch?v=zJSUTTSAEKo

17 Josef Mengele's Wikipedia page elaborates on his war crimes: https://en.wikipedia.org/wiki/Josef_Mengele

18 In this video for Holocaust Education Week in 2020, my voiceover starts at the 16:54 mark: https://virtualjcc.com/watch/opening-night-stream-holocaust-education-week-nov2

Chapter Six: Broken Homes

19 An image of the building when it was Mount Sinai can be found on the hospital's "Our History" page here: https://www.mountsinai.on.ca/about_us/history

20 Read more about the Big Brothers Big Sisters program on their website at: https://bigbrothersbigsisters.ca

Chapter Seven: Walking Away from My Dream

21 The Don Henley song "Dirty Laundry" provides the soundtrack to a compilation of news anchors in this video: https://www.youtube.com/watch?v=ju_GLKaH4vM

22 When I left CITY-TV, the station aired a blooper tape of mine. It's at the 43:50 mark in this video and is good for a laugh: https://www.youtube.com/watch?v=31vzdExKs3U

Chapter Nine: Book Writing, Ventures, and Misadventures

23 My book *When the Headline is You: An Insider's Guide to Handling the Media* can be purchased on Amazon at: https://www.amazon.com/dp/0470543949

Chapter Ten: Getting into Harvard

24 FBI Director James Comey's remarks at the 2015 IACP conference can be listened to at the following link: https://www.fbi.gov/audio-repository/news-speeches-comey-at-2015-iacp-conference.mp3/view

Chapter Eleven: Political Encounters

25 Learn more about Kennedy's famous rocking chair here: https://www.jfkmemorabilia.com/john-f-kennedy-research/the-famous-kennedy-rocker.html

Chapter Twelve: Celebrity Encounters

26 Eddie Griffin's complete filmography can be viewed on IMDB: https://www.imdb.com/name/nm0341176/

27 Listen to the phone message that José Feliciano left for my wife, Annie here on the Who I am After All YouTube channel: https://youtu.be/sLzfvSGxhso

28 An image of David Beckham's impressive neck tattoos can be found in this article: https://www.mirror.co.uk/3am/celebrity-news/david-beckham-shows-new-tattoo-12457202

29 The *Wall Street Journal* article about Keith Harrell can be found here: https://www.wsj.com/articles/SB920338096472349500

Chapter Fourteen: Gratitude

30 An English translation and history of the Mourner's Kaddish can be found on its Wikipedia page: https://en.wikipedia.org/wiki/Kaddish

31 The image of Kim Phúc is on the AP Images site here:http://www.apimages.com/Collection/Landing/Photographer-Nick-Ut-The-Napalm-Girl-/ebfc0a860aa946ba9e77eb786d46207e

32 Kim Phúc's article in *Christianity Today* can be read here: https://www.christianitytoday.com/ct/2018/may/napalm-girl-kim-phuc-phan-thi-fire-road.html

33 A recent CBC Interview with Kim Phúc can be viewed here: https://www.youtube.com/watch?v=SWH2Vi0Pcol

Chapter Sixteen: After All

34 The music video for "Don't You (Forget About Me)" by Simple Minds is here: https://www.youtube.com/watch?v=CdqoNKCCt7A

35 The music video for "Don't Forget Me When I'm Gone" by Glass Tiger is here: https://www.youtube.com/watch?v=JG2IFsz_n5c

36 The audio for "Turn! Turn! Turn!" by The Byrds is here: https://www.youtube.com/watch?v=xVOJla2vYx8

37 The audio for "O-o-h Child" by The Five Stairsteps is here: https://www.youtube.com/watch?v=dguz0IsCuKU

38 Details about Lynda Fishman's book *Repairing Rainbows* can be found at: https://repairingrainbows.com/

39 Lynda Fishman's blog post about Gratitude is here: http://www.repairingrainbows.com/blog/?p=27

40 Jonathan Goldstein's Podcast episode on *Heavyweight* about Buzzie and Sheldon is here: https://gimletmedia.com/shows/heavyweight/94hwad

CPSIA information can be obtained
at www.ICGtesting.com
Printed in the USA
BVHW070919310123
657438BV00002B/258